# THE "NEW"
# SOLAR RETURN
# BOOK
## of
# PREDICTION

# THE "NEW"
# SOLAR RETURN
# BOOK
# of
# PREDICTION

# RAYMOND A. MERRIMAN

Seek-It Publications  P.O. Box 250012  W. Bloomfield, MI USA

# DEDICATION TO SECOND BOOK

*This book is dedicated to Denise Wilson-Cowing, who loves and respects the value of solar returns as much as I do. Like myself, she has spent three decades calculating - and then traveling to - "the optimal astrological location" on the birth dates of both her spouse and herself, in order to attain the "most desirable" solar return chart for that year. For us, solar return travels have become an annual pilgrimage. We approach each year with awe and wonderment of the Universal order, and thankfulness for the privilege and freedom to apply this sacred knowledge.*

1st printing ...   December, 1977
2nd printing ..   March, 1978
3rd printing ...   September, 1979
4th printing ...   May, 1981
5th printing ...   December, 1982
6th printing ...   October, 1986
7th printing ...   November, 1988
8th printing ...   March, 1992
9th printing ...   March, 1998 - 1st of "NEW" edition
10th printing ... March, 2000 - 2nd of "NEW" edition
11th printing ... June, 2009 - 3rd of the "NEW" edition

**ISBN 0-930-706-34-X**

THE "NEW" SOLAR RETURN BOOK OF PREDICTION

Copyright © 1977 by Seek-It Publications
 P.O. Box 250012 W. Bloomfield, MI. 48325
 248-626-3034   Fax 248-626-5674
 e-mail: mmacycles@msn.com
 internet: mmacycles.com

Printed in the United States of America
Library of Congress Catalog No: 77-84541

Cover Design by Cheryl Gaboski
Charts used herein are from the Pathfinder Astrology System.

# TABLE OF CONTENTS

## THE VIEW OF THE YEAR

## TIMING EVENTS FOR THE YEAR

# INTRODUCTION TO "NEW" BOOK ON SOLAR RETURNS

It has now been 21 years since I wrote the first book on solar returns. I know that for a fact because to this day my wife still kids me about writing this book on our first honeymoon - and we just celebrated our 21st anniversary. The story is an interesting one (I think), and since so many readers have commented favorably on the original book's "Dedication" (which is repeated herein), I will now - in the words of Paul Harvey - "tell the real story" behind that dedication.

In early 1976, I was a wild, crazy, and heart-broken astrologer. I had just broken up with a beautiful woman from Hawaii who had successfully convinced me that she was - really - the love of my life. But like all "loves of one's life", she drove me crazy and I drove her down south, where the warm winds blow and the ocean breezes have been known to cure all kinds of silly human ailments .... but it didn't work. I wouldn't marry her because marriage was the last thing on the mind of this wild child of the stars. Heck, I hadn't even had a Saturn return yet! It was a no-brainer: I chose heartbreak, poetry, and astrology to a life of promised marital bliss.

That decision led me into the worst and best of times. Because this decision wasn't truly a no-brainer, but rather the type that leads one onto a dark journey, into the murky pits of one's true identity - wondering what he really wants out of life, what he's really willing to give to life to get it, and whether or not he really has the "stuff" within himself to make it happen - I spent a lot of time in study, reflection, and meditation.

The result was that I traveled to New Mexico - alone - for my birthdate on Christmas (yes, that's right, I am one of those fortunate Christmas babies). The story of that is described in Chapter One: Introduction to Solar Returns. It describes how I then met my "wife-to-be", the one I am celebrating our 21st anniversary with as I write this Solar Return Book Two.

But back to the subject... it is an interesting story, even if it is my own. So something happened during 1976. I had my Saturn return that summer, and it was a very good one. The week before it happened I spoke for the first time at an AFA (American Federation of Astrologers) convention in Las Vegas. It was great. I received invitations to speak all over the country, which for a 29-year old with ruling planet Mercury in Sagittarius like myself, was like breaking the Pinyata. A week later, at the exact time of my Saturn return, I was comfortably sitting high atop a mountain just outside Malibu, California (how appropriate for a Capricorn to celebrate his first Saturn return). I had, in a sense, climbed a mountain professionally. Astrologers and students of astrology responded favorably to my work.

But back to the subject.... it is an interesting story that really leads somewhere related to the subject of this book. Did I ever say how much I loved to travel, especially to those warm and sunny beaches in areas that many consider paradise.... So I've started dating this beautiful girl that I met in Chapter One of this book at rather irregular intervals between my trips. The problem is: I'm falling in love with her - and then leaving for another speaking trip. These were the best of times and worst of times... (who said that?)... loving, then leaving, then coming home, loving, leaving, then coming home... urrrgggghhh. The loving kept getting better, and with Saturn return in effect, biological-like changes were happening in my consciousness. It was like the internal "Cosmic Clock" was striking an important hour in the cycle of this cosmic cowboy, and rather than riding off again into the sunset of yet another metaphysical adventure down south (where the sandy white siren beaches reach out for my ethereal hand in a never ending fertility dance)... hold it just a moment here!

"Whoa", I said. I said to myself, cuz I didn't want to admit it to anyone else, "I think I'm really too far in love. I wanna be with her, and I'm going away again, and again ..... and I wonder if she feels the same way about me?" In fact, I was already gone - in Florida - when I had this conversation with myself.

Well, one of the characteristics about having a ruling planet like Mercury in Sagittarius is that you don't beat around the bush... if you know what I mean. So I called her up and said something like: "Debby, why don't you go get a blood test, come on down here and let's get married, go on a honeymoon to the Virgin Islands, then go back home and tell everyone we've gotten engaged, to get married in May?" I'm thinking that will give me enough time to get used to the message my cosmic/biological clock was trying to tell me but what my mind just wasn't accepting delivery on.

So she did. Now, before you think that this was an easy feat, you must consider a very important fact. This lady is a Leo who has Saturn rising in Virgo. She is not one given to quick nor rash judgments. So since she agreed, I figured two things: 1) she does love me, and 2) it must be the right thing to do because she doesn't make mistakes (at least none she'll ever admit to).

Now you're probably wondering..... "Ray, what does this have to do with Solar Return Book Two?" Well, I'm glad you asked (or was it I who asked?), because like I say..... it's an interesting story. So Debby (that's her name) flies down to Disney World (I mean, is that appropriate for one like myself who has Neptune rising and Pisces ruling the 7th house?), and we drive down to spend the night at one Josephine Sabino's incredible "garden house" in Miami, and the next morning Josephine marries us under a banana tree and we're off to a honeymoon in the Virgin Islands.

The date we got secretly married was December 4, 1976. The Sun was in Sagittarius and the Moon was conjunct Jupiter in Taurus. Josephine said if we got married with the Moon in Taurus it would be forever (did I mention these were the best and worst of times????...). There are probably several things I did not mention... but let me tell you how this plays out. It is an interesting story. When I took this trip down south, I did in fact plan to go to the Virgin Islands ..... to write, but not as part of a honeymoon.

Earl and Audrey were dear friends of mine. Audrey, like myself, was a traveling nomad, and we had been to some very interesting places together (the most interesting might have been a trip down the Orinoco River through the jungles in central Venezuela, but that's another story). Her husband Earl worked for the FDIC (Federal Deposit Insurance Corporation). He had been sent to the Virgin Islands to investigate some shady banking practices, and whenever he was sent somewhere interesting, Audrey always invited me to visit - which of course, being that my natal Mercury is in Sagittarius, I always obliged. Interestingly enough, the place Audrey and Earl holed up was called the "Watergate" Villas. In 1976, that was a hot name for an apartment complex!!! Yup, same group for which President Nixon became infamous.

So, the point. Did I ever mention that I have a Sun and Moon in Capricorn? I wrote the *Solar Return Book of Prediction* on my honeymoon. Every morning I would wake up, go into the office room of their Watergate Villas, and type away until noon, after which time Debby, Audrey, and I would drive into town and participate in the island holiday celebrations until Earl was done investigatin', and then we'd go party some more into the evening.

So that's the story. And now here are the relevant facts. Every 19 years the Sun and Moon return to their same positions on the same day. It's always an interesting solar return (the 19th of anything), because it is also close to a lunar Nodal return. So in December, 1995, 19 years after I wrote the original *Solar Return Book*, I started to redo the book during its Nodal return. And now it is 21st solar return of my original wedding date as I finish this revision. And to this day, my beautiful wife Debra continues to remind me: "Do I remember our honeymoon? All you did on our honeymoon was write that damn book!" I thought it was a great honeymoon. She thought all I did was work. So I married her again on May 18, 1977, and for our honeymoon we went to Philadelphia - where I worked. But don't despair. Two months later we went to Hawaii where we played.... ahhh, these were the best of times and the worst....

Thank God for solar returns. With them each year comes a new adventure. And the opportunity to travel to distant lands where ocean breezes and sandy white beaches call... for a time, and a purpose, that is timeless. One's solar return is precious. It is a sacred day. It is the one time of the astrological year when one is in synch with the center of the solar system, the creative force of life itself.

Now you might be wondering what's different about this book than the original book. Well for one thing, this book costs more (yes, my dear friends, the price of paper has indeed increased a lot in 21 years, not to mention the value we place upon our services and time). But that is not all that is different. The original book spent a considerable effort delineating the overall tone of the year - interpreting the solar return chart itself. It spent a goodly amount of time outlining unique timing factors that can be applied to the solar return chart - things like progressing the solar return moon to both the solar return and natal planets, and the now famous "One-Degree-Per-Day" Progressed solar return angles, to both the solar return and natal chart. In spite of the fact that those techniques were described, there was very little delineation of those meanings. This new book adds this much-wanted element: it delineates the meaning of those times when the "Progressed solar return Moon and angles" actually aspect the solar return and natal planets, thus providing a chronological guide on "what and when" to expect things during the course of one's birth year. This new feature alone makes this a potentially valuable reference guide, and one that is not available anywhere else - except in the software program of the same name.

Did I mention the software program? The new *Raymond A. Merriman Solar Return software program by Matrix?* Well it's available too (through Seek-It Publications, no less - see back page of this book for more information). At the stroke of a couple of keyboard buttons, you can now print out these dates, in chronological order - *with interpretations* - for the year. Of course nothing beats reading the book for learning to do it on your own, but we are moving rapidly into the age of telecommunication advances and cyberspace, and tools such as solar return software will be efficient and valuable..... but if you want to know *the rest of the story* about how solar returns (ala Merriman) began, let go back to the original work....

# DEDICATION FROM THE
# ORIGINAL BOOK

A dedication is an author's prerogative. How he handles it is also his prerogative (especially if he is his own publisher). So bear with me, dear reader, as I exercise my prerogative in writing this dedication, which is one of the very few places in the book where I can speak to you - or anyone - in the first person gender!

In the cold winter's months when those of us who live where it truly feels cold in the winter's months like to dream ... and dream ... of warm ocean breezes on a bright sandy-white beach somewhere in paradise ... the Sun can be very special.

For one who is observant of his relationship to the forces of nature, the Sun is different in its effect to an individual upon Earth at different points in time and space. Truly: in the winter (especially in the north) the Sun feels different than in the summer, and the individual responds differently in each season. In the areas near the equator (especially on those islands where indeed there are ocean breezes on sandy-white, sunny beaches) the Sun also feels different (regardless of time since it is hardly noticed anyway in these climates) than in those areas far away from the equator.

So the relationship of Man to time and space will effect his relationship to the Sun. The reverse may also be true (as those of us who have experienced those ocean breezes on the sandy-white, sunny paradise beaches know), that the relationship of Man to the Sun will effect his relationship to time and space (particularly time). Which is to say: that the Earth/Sun relationship *can be* very special to Man (both sexes included in this term).

7

As the reader might suspect by now, the Earth/Sun relationship is very special to this author. Not just in an astrological-intellectual sense (as in the case of examining the Sun's position in the horoscope - which is very interesting indeed to me), but also in a physical sense. For one thing, the Sun does indeed affect me differently given variations in time (of year) and space (location upon Earth). Physically I feel different when these conditions are altered. But also - and perhaps more significant to those who are Mercurial or Uranian in nature as I am - I *perceive* life differently given variations in these same two conditions. Those who have never traveled upon *this* plane may never know what I am talking about. Those who have traveled but never halted to examine what is going on between themselves and nature, may never believe what I am talking about. Those who have never relaxed on a tropical paradise island where indeed there are soothing ocean breezes on sandy-white, secluded beaches, may never experience what I am talking about.

Before I continue with this simple dedication which at this point may seem to lead to nowhere, let me share a couple of things I have heard along the way. Somewhere I read a study that indicated people in warmer climates tend to live longer than those who reside in cold climates. It seems that the study reported that those who live in Hawaii have a longer life expectancy than anywhere else in the United States. It seems that somewhere I also read a study that the oldest living beings upon our planet (many believed to be centurians) are located somewhere in Russia, and the supposed reason for their longevity lies in their simple-but-pure diet. It seems to me that variations in diet and climate might effect one's life span upon Earth. The point is - if indeed there is any point to this dedication at all and I didn't really promise a point, only the belief I had that it is my prerogative to write a dedication - that a harmonious between Man and Nature (which includes Man's relationship to the Sun and those things which the Sun gives life to), whereby Man does not struggle against the elements of nature, may result in a longer (and perhaps happier) life. Perhaps. Just perhaps. I can't prove it. It just seems logical.

"So what," you ask, "does all of this have to do with a dedication to a book on astrology?" Well, several things. To begin with - which is *not* a good way to begin a sentence - I am frustrated. That's right, frustrated! "Huh? What's he talking about now?" you ask. I'll tell you. As one who has studied creative writing for a number of years while in college (although after reading this book many of you may not believe this statement: it's like astrology and health - if you don't use it you lose it... or was that sex???), I am perfectly aware that a "dedication" is proper to include in almost any sort of book. I also realize, as a practical human being (lots of prominent Earth), that very few people ever care about or read a dedication. I therefore *knew* that here - and nowhere else in this book - I could unleash my uncanny abilities as a creative writer, that here I could "take a chance", and nobody would ever notice! Nobody, that is, except those few of you whom I trust to preserve this secret: that I am really, deep down, a frustrated, creative writer. So to you I say: "Congratulations!" Why? Why not? If a Leo woman can congratulate her husband on his choice of mates (thanks Karma Welch for that one) in this lifetime, then a writer can congratulate his readers for bearing through what might seem to be overbearing creativity!

This book commenced late in the afternoon of November 24th, 1976, as the Moon very quietly entered union with the Goat (a union which concluded with its trine to Jupiter in Taurus). It was due to the good graces of Josephine Sabino, to whom this dedication begins, that I was able to initiate this work. She and her family left for the day. That was in Miami, Florida for anyone who wishes to cast an electional chart. I did. That's why I believe this book will do well. Anyway, Mrs. Sabino is one of a new breed of astrologers: she is organic in both diet and thought. There are two other reasons why I dedicate this book first of all to Mrs. Sabino: she has served as a source of infinite inspiration in my work, and she also advised my wife on "what a good wife is."

For those who do not know, or who might even be a little uncertain, there are lands to the south, far, far away to the south of

9

Florida. Lands where pirates once roamed and ships stocked to the gills with treasures for the Queen oftentimes sank. Lands of buried treasures, where legends and superstitions that would scare and intrigue even the coldest and hardest of souls. Lands where you can step to the edge of the World and see nothing but more water and wonder .... wonder if there is anything out there anymore but more and more water. These are the areas, the lands, the islands, that we of the north dream of so frequently in the winter, for here lie the sandy-white beaches where soothing ocean breezes constantly blow. Here lie the Virgin Islands, a group of little hilltops whose land is mostly covered by the oceans of the Earth. One of these, St. Thomas, is rather well-known. But off on peninsula known as Bolongo Bay, where the jutted cliffs drop sharply into the sea where waves smash mightily against rock, sits a very quiet village indeed. And in this village live two Americans who are accepted by the natives of the island - Earl and Audrey. In attitude and appearance, they are both ageless and young. It is because of their kindness and openness that I had the opportunity to write the greater body of this book in a place with no distractions. To both of them, this book is also dedicated.

Back up north, work had to be done. The editing, typing, and re-writing, were formidable tasks. Especially in the winter when we of the north dream of those sandy-white beaches and soft ocean breezes. But work had to be done on this book, and for that I chose a Capricorn and a Taurus. It didn't matter that I chose my sister and mother, but that I chose one - or two in this case - who knew how to edit and type. They (Joan, my Capricorn sister, and Norma, my Taurus mother - I also have a Virgo father, but he spends his days tuning the family TV) did as much work on the book as anyone. And to them I am very grateful. Someday I hope they can spend time where it is warm so they will know what I am talking about.

And alas, to the lady who shared the entire experience of creating, re-creating, living and re-living this book with me, from beginning to end and re-beginning to re-end, I also dedicate this book: Debby Christy-Merriman.

This then concludes my dedication. Oh, I know you probably think I copped out by not going through with the creative stuff, but you must understand dear reader that this is after all a very serious and technical book. And with a book such as this, one who likes to write creatively can become a little frustrated by the literary restrictions necessary to convey "techniques" and "methods." So a writer such as myself must make use of whatever space is available, whether it is before or after the content of the book (and in this case, both), to "let it out." So to all of you who have ever "let it out", and even to those of you who are still thinking of "letting it out", and even to those of you who have nothing to really let out because you're not really keeping anything in (or its so far down that you haven't begun to realize it's even there at all) ... to all of you fine people whom I have met along my travels ... this book is dedicated to you.

# 1. CHAPTER ONE

# INTRODUCTION TO SOLAR RETURNS

This book, as the name implies, is *about* prediction. Using astrology - in particular, the solar return horoscope of an individual - specific techniques which can be of invaluable service to the astrological consultant are clearly spelled out in this text. Some of these techniques are old (perhaps as old as astrology itself) while others are new (or at least to the author's knowledge, they are new), but in either case it seems that as a form of prognostication, they offer perhaps the most accurate of all astrological tools.

The technique of using solar returns as a predictive method has long been acknowledged by the astrological community. Yet very little literature is available on the subject. This may be due to the fact that very few astrologers use solar returns in their practice because it involves setting up an additional chart. It may be due to the fact that quite often a solar return chart seems to merely confirm what progressions and transits already indicate. In the latter case, this may be so when using conventional means of interpreting the solar return chart as outlined in the available literature on the subject. But when used with the natal planets, when techniques of progressing the solar return chart are implemented as well as examining transits to it, it will be found that indeed the solar return chart offers one of the most inclusive and accurate means of forecasting-- considerably more than the examination of progressions and transits to the natal chart alone!

This subject is about prediction. As most astrologers understand, it is nearly impossible to predict an exact event in any person's life. The nature of the event, or change, shown by the aspecting planets and angles, is often possible. The areas of life where changes occur,

12

shown by the house emphasis of planets involved, is also quite possible. The timing of the change is the forte upon which the astrologer stands, for this is almost universally accurate when applying proper astrological methods. But determining with accuracy the exact event by means of horoscopy is a never-ending quest pursued by many, achieved by very few (if any). Why events are impossible to predict with exactness all the time is a moot point of controversy. It may lie in the assumption that an individual maintains an element of self-determinism and free-will. It may lie in the theory that each individual has a different spiritual (karmic) pattern to unfold despite the similarity of planetary make-up. Or it might lie in the fact that the same planet has such a wide variety of influences within its nature.

This text (or any text for that matter) cannot answer this dilemma about prediction. As with any other science, astrology and its proponents must use a number of variables - both directly and indirectly related to Astrology per se - to make educated judgments as to "what might happen." If we go outside of astrology and determine the conditions existing in the lives and backgrounds of each, then even greater accuracy is possible in prognosticating what change one may undergo. And even then there is still a variety of directions that a planet's influence may undertake. The point, though, is this: the more refined your tools, and the more relevant information you have, the greater your accuracy in forecasting is likely to be.

The purpose of this book is to provide the astrologer with finer tools in the art of forecasting, and you - the client - with a more accurate description of what issues are currently unfolding in your life. It does not purport to be the final, or omnipotent, word in the matter of forecasting, for as long as we are human beings still striving for perfection and realization, there will never be an end in this matter. No, instead we will just continue becoming - becoming closer and closer, better and better at what we do and how we do it. Hopefully this book is a step in that direction.

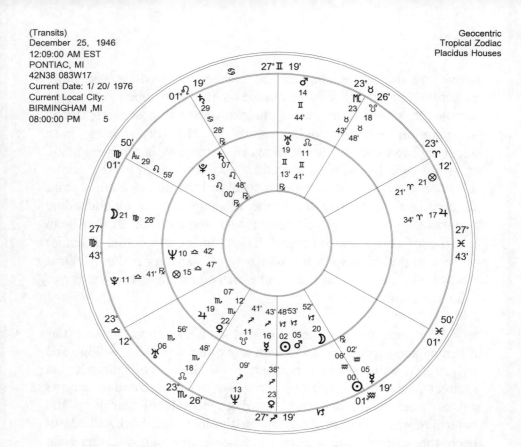

**Figure 1: Author's natal chart (inner wheel) and transits (outer wheel) at time of meeting wife-to-be.**

The author's own personal interest in the solar return chart began some years ago in an attempt to find the astrological correlate to first time of meeting my wife-to-be. Admittedly, as is quite often the case, major transits were in effect, aspecting natal planets (see Figure 1). Transiting Pluto in the first house was conjunct natal Neptune, ruler of the 7th house; transiting Neptune was in trine to natal Pluto; and transiting Jupiter was in the seventh house separating from a trine to natal Mercury, ruler of the chart. The first two conditions would be in effect for several months - even a couple of years - so they did not satisfy my curiosity for an exact timing. Jupiter's transit during the same period seemed to provide the exactness sought, except that its trine to Mercury was the third such passage in the last year, due to the retrograde factor.

It would seem that the first two periods - and especially the first - of the three transiting trines would have been stronger, and in retrospect it is true that those times too ushered in significant relationships, though none as significant as the third.

The search for further astrological correlation led to the exploration of the solar return chart for that year (see Figure 2). In this horoscope the Moon, representing significant relationships, is posited in the first house of personal affairs; Jupiter, the planet representing favorable unions, is strongly positioned in the 7th house (and co-ruler of it, and in trine to the other co-ruler, Neptune) of partnerships; and Venus, natural ruler of the seventh house and partnerships, in nearly in exact trine to the cusp of the Descendant. The Moon's North Node was also conjunct Venus, and both the North Node and Venus of the solar return chart were in conjunction to the author's natal Venus conjunct Pluto. The solar return chart was thus conducive for a year in which favorable, significant relationships could be formed.

Yet the timing of the "first meeting" event is even more amazing. With only scant information available on the timing of events via the solar return chart (with the exception perhaps of the Key Cycle technique), I began experimenting with a number of theoretical possibilities. It seemed to me that if the solar return set up conditions for a one year period, then it was very similar to the method of progressions wherein "one day equals one year" of life. In other words, in the 24-hour period following the return of the Sun to its natal placement - for any given year - lies an astrological outline of what the next year portends - just like the method used in secondary progressions. Even the commonly accepted method of progressing the solar return Moon (discussed in this book) is the same calculation used for progressing the natal Moon.

Thus the theoretical basis of solar returns was clear: the transits in a 24-hour period following the return of the Sun to its natal position provided a structure (horoscope) for experience within the

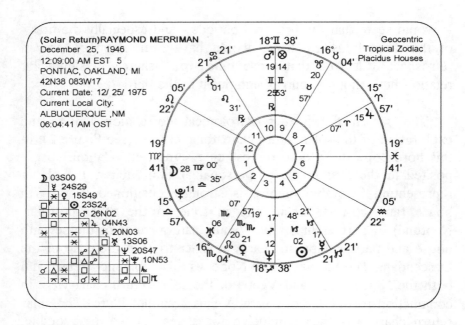

**Figure 2: Author's solar return for year he met his wife-to-be. Took place in Albuquerque, New Mexico on December 24, 1975**

following twelve months. By dividing the daily motion of each of the planets and angles by 12 (months) or 365 days, one could determine the monthly and even daily positions of each. Obviously the division of each of the planets' daily motion by the number of days in a year yielded a very minute motion, but the division of the angles by this factor - particularly the meridian - was very plausible. It was so plausible that it seemed strange that nothing had ever been written on this subject.

The "one degree per day angular progression method" is theoretically sound. If indeed the 24 hours following the moment of one's solar return sets up conditions (astrologically) for the following year, then the angles which move 360 degrees in 24 hours (or one day) do progress at the rate of approximately one degree per day. This is close to constant when dealing with the meridian angles, and more variable with the horizon.

Applying this "one degree per day angular progression method" to my own solar return chart was fascinating. The meeting of my "wife-to-be" mentioned previously occurred on January 20, 1976, 27 days after the solar return. Progressing the solar return Midheaven (based on the location of the solar return, not the residence or birth place) forward 27 degrees yielded a 15 degree Aries Descendant for the date of the first meeting - exactly conjunct the solar return Jupiter that was posited in the seventh house!

The accuracy of this one event prompted an intense investigation of all the solar return angles to the solar return and natal planets. Over and over again the results clicked with what was going on in my life at each time, according to the planets and angles being aspected. The research extended to the horoscopes of friends, then clients, each time confirming with surprising accuracy (to the day in most cases, and within three days in almost all cases) an event or phenomenon which occurred in that individual's life.

### THE IMPORTANCE OF "BEING THERE ON TIME"

As stated in the first line in this chapter, this book is about prediction. *Astrology is a study whose calculations depend upon a specific time in a particular space.* It only works in a time and space dimension. The moment of the solar return occurs at only one exact instance each year, and usually that is on or within one day of one's birth date. At that exact moment, the Earth is in exactly the same position in its orbit around the Sun that existed at the moment of one's birth. Viewed from the perspective of astrology, the transiting Sun is in exactly the same degree, minute, and second of arc as it was in the natal horoscope. Thus that "moment in time" each year is the time from which the solar return chart is calculated.

But just as important as is the time of the solar return, so too is the location of the person at that moment. Somewhere upon Earth, it is noon at the moment of one's solar return. Somewhere else, it is sunrise, or sunset, or any other time. The exact moment of time is a "star time" (or sidereal time), but the "clock time" can vary depending upon which time zone the native is physically in. And herein lies one of the great debates in astrology: which location do you use to construct a solar return chart? The place of residence, the place of birth, or the place where the native is located at that very moment? It is the author's belief - and this is supported by many years of observation - that the latter is the correct answer. The location of the person at that moment becomes the "place"` to use for calculating the solar return chart.

To use any other location except where the person is at that exact moment is a violation of the fundamental precept of astrology. For an event to have a horoscope, one must use the exact time *and* location of that event. The solar return moment is such an event. It takes place at a specific time. To whom it effects is obviously of significance. Where that person (to whom the event is relevant) is located is also of extreme importance. That is the location for the event, upon which a correct horoscope is cast.

To construct a horoscope upon any other location (than that of where the native to whom the event is relevant is located) would be akin to constructing a horoscope of a marriage, or the start of business, based upon the birth place of the individuals involved, rather than the location of the marriage or place of business. They may be hundreds - even thousands - of miles apart! It would be akin to asking a horary question, such as "Will I find the lost article in this hotel on my vacation?" based upon the place of one's birth or residence, and not the hotel that is 5000 miles away. The event is taking place here, not there. And where the event actually takes place determines the coordinates to use for the construction of the relevant horoscope. It is that simple. Either you believe Astrology works on the basis of time *and* space, or you don't. Either you believe in time as a factor of *both* the Earth in its orbit around the Sun, and the Earth rotating on its own axes to produce day *and* night, or you don't.

So there is a consciousness that can be effected based upon one's solar return: a consciousness of time and place. The time one

18

cannot alter. It ties into one's biological clock set at the moment of birth. It can be calculated with exact precision each year. However, one has a choice in determining the *place*. If one knows ahead of time, exactly when (star time) the solar return is to take place, then one can choose any location to be in at that time. Depending upon where one chooses to be, the clock time may differ. It may be noon in one time zone, or one hour earlier in the next, or several hours earlier or later depending upon how far away one wishes to be at that moment. Or more likely, depending upon what rising and culminating signs (and degrees) one wishes to set up for the next year's solar return horoscope.

Thus knowledge of solar returns can effect a certain consciousness of time and space. One has the opportunity - through use of his/her knowledge - to create an applicable horoscope that will be in effect for one year. The key phrase here is horoscope, as it pertains to angles and houses. Obviously one cannot change the zodiacal positions of the planets in effect at the time of the return. But one can change the degrees and signs of the horizon (angles) and hence house cusps, and hence houses that the planets will be posited in at the time of the solar return. And to do so means that one has chosen a certain consciousness about that time and that place related to that time. It becomes the basis for a sacred act, a pilgrimage, an annual mission of significance only to you, a "holy event" dealing with your own personal relationship to the Infinite.

The exact time of one's solar return is a sacred annual event for each individual. It happens at only one specific moment each year. It is at that moment - and only that moment - in which the Earth/Sun relationship are exactly the same as when you were born. Such a moment constitutes an "event", and as with all events, this one too is the basis for a horoscope of import.

However the importance of this horoscope is unique only to the individual to whom it applies. The quality of that "moment" (i.e. the time of one's solar return) becomes the "seed" of that annual cycle. It is the basis for a horoscope that will describe the

19

astrological factors in effect for that one-year cycle. A "moment" of such importance favors a certain mind-set of the individual as it occurs. This is especially true if one accepts the premise that thought creates (or influences) reality. If every moment of time has its own unique quality, then one would want the "quality" of the solar return "moment" to be special in a favorable way, especially since it becomes the horoscope for the year in that person's life.

Given this premise, the individual is encouraged to enter the solar return moment with a sense of reverence. The individual is encouraged to put some thought and effort into assuring that this moment is somehow empowered, infused with an energy or thoughts consistent with what that individual would want to experience in the coming year.

What should one do at this moment? That of course is up to each individual (you). Obviously it would not be a favorable omen if one engaged in an argument, or sat home brooding, or went to work in an atmosphere of frustration or boredom. Such experiences at the time of one's solar return would likely set the foundation for a mind-set for the entire year - and it would be negative.

The following ideas are intended only as suggestions. They take into account the premise that one's solar return is the most personally sacred of all days of the year. Therefore, going into the moment of a solar return, one is advised to plan something special, something ideally that would "empower" that moment . A ritual of some sort might be a good idea.

For instance, you might take into account your location-to-be at that moment. Choose someplace special, a place in which you are comfortable, happy, and in harmony with. Perhaps it is near a lake, ocean, river, or mountain. Perhaps it is on a beach or in a forest. Or perhaps it is in a favorite room.

Set the "stage". Perhaps you wish to light a candle, and/or play music. Perhaps the direction you are facing (North, East, West or

South - facing the Sun, or the Moon) has special meaning to you. Perhaps there are artifacts (i.e. pets, jewelry, stones) that have personal meaning, and you wish to display them in your "circle." Perhaps there is a special person whom you have decided to share this moment with.

The setting (if effected) should be completely set at least ten minutes prior to the solar return moment. As you enter the 10-minute time band leading into the solar return moment, you may consider beginning a meditation. How one meditates is completely individualistic. Perhaps you prefer to just enter a very relaxed state. Perhaps you wish to chant. Perhaps you use visualization or affirmation exercises. If the latter, then after achieving a state of relaxation, you might visualize the areas of interest coming up in the next year. In this visualization exercise, you might try to see yourself as happy and successful in each situation.

This meditation, or contemplation, should last into - and slightly beyond - the solar return moment. Once the moment has passed, and the meditation is complete, you are encouraged to give thanks. This may done in a prayer, or whatever form is sacred to you. In this way, you bring a gentle closure to the sacred moment which has just passed, a moment which has now become the foundation for the one-year cycle about to begin.

You cannot be late for this moment. Otherwise, you might be symbolically late throughout the entire year. Do not take this moment in time lightly. Otherwise, all of your affairs may be symbolically taken lightly all year. The solar return is best viewed in the spirit of a pilgrimage, or a mission. It is the most important "holiday" of the year to you. It is the one time during the year that you are "connected" to the Infinite through the special relationship of the Earth and Sun. It is a moment when you are potentially in tune with your destiny, which is signified by the Earth/Sun relationship. The Sun is what you are becoming (the future, your growth potential). The Earth is where you have incarnated (present, your being). Give it the reverence it is due.

# 2. CHAPTER TWO

## CALCULATING THE SOLAR RETURN

Perhaps more than any other facet of Astrology, exactness and accuracy of calculation are essential in the construction and interpretation of the solar return chart. Without the exact time of birth, natal charts (such as a solar chart or an Aries flat chart) can still be constructed and interpreted, though not with the same degree of accuracy if the birth time is known. A solar return chart, however, cannot be constructed if the birth moment is unknown. Not only is the exact time of birth necessary, but so too is the exact longitudinal position of the Sun - to the degree, minute and second! Many astrologers calculate the solar return only to the nearest minute of solar longitude, and since the Sun's movement is about one minute of arc every twenty-four minutes of time, the moment of the solar return may be off several minutes. Consequently the houses - and most importantly the angles - may be incorrect by several degrees! This could not only alter the interpretation of the chart, but also the timing of events and significant personal issues according to techniques outlined in this book.

Several books are already in print instructing the calculation of the solar return chart by various methods. However, many astrologers now have at their disposal software programs which can accurately and quickly calculate solar return charts. Thus this chapter on "How To Calculate A Solar Return Chart" may be unnecessary to many.

Since most books instruct the calculation of the solar return chart by means of logarithms, and we do not wish to repeat those works, this book will instruct via the proportion method. Besides, with the familiarity and availability of the hand calculator in today's world, the proportion method can be calculated perhaps easier than the logarithm method.

Construction of the solar return horoscope is a two-part process. First, one must determine to the nearest second the longitudinal position of the natal Sun. Second, one must determine to the nearest minute of time that moment of the Sun's return to its natal sign, degree, minute and second of arc - and then construct a horoscope for this time. This will usually occur within one day of an individual's birthdate. In actuality, the time of the solar return is about six hours later each year, and with leap year every fourth year, the 24-hour difference is made up.

In the case of finding one's natal Sun to the nearest degree, minute and second of arc, instructions will be given for both the midnight and noon ephemerides, since the noon ephemeris seems more available prior to 1950. In the case of determining the exact time of a solar return though, we will use only the midnight ephemeris in the example. In both cases, Greenwich Mean Time (GMT) will be the standard referred to in calculations.

*FINDING THE NATAL SUN*

1. *Determining the Longitudinal Position of the Natal Sun:* (using a midnight ephemeris):

A. Determine the Greenwich Mean Time (GMT) of birth.

B. Determine how many hours and minutes this is removed from midnight on the GMT birth date. *Reduce to total minutes.* This become *a* of proportion below.

C. Let *b* of proportion be *1440 minutes* - the number of minutes in a 24-hour day (60' x 24 hrs).

23

D. Determine the daily motion of the Sun:

     1. Subtract the midnight position of the Sun, on GMT birthdate, from midnight position of Sun on day *after* birthdate. Use degree, minute and *second* of each.

     2. Reduce result to total *seconds*. Result should always be near 3660 seconds (average daily motion of Sun is about one degree, or 60 minutes, or 60 x 60 = 3600 seconds).

     Let this result be *d* of proportion given below.

     E. Determine the exact longitudinal position of natal Sun, using the following proportion:

$$\frac{a}{b} = \frac{c}{d}$$

wherein:

     a = Total number of minutes GMT of birth is removed from midnight (Step B).

     b = Total number of minutes in a 24-hour day, or 1440 (Step C).

     c = Distance the Sun has moved from midnight to GMT of birth, on GMT date of birth.

     d = Daily motion of Sun on GMT date of birth (Step D).

     1. *c*, the unknown can be determined by the following:

$$c = \frac{a \times d}{b}$$

This will give the distance the Sun traveled (actually the Earth in relation to the Sun) between midnight on the GMT date of birth, to the exact Greenwich Mean Time of birth.

24

2. The result will be in total *seconds*. Convert back into minutes if result is over 60 seconds. (Do this by dividing result by 60). This gives you minutes, and the remainder is the number of seconds.

3. *Add* this result to the midnight position of the Sun given on the GMT date of birth. *This, then, is the natal longitude of the Sun, to the nearest degree, minute, and second of arc.*

Those using a hand calculator based on the number 10 decimal system (and most are) must remember to convert decimals back into a minutes and seconds system based on the number 60. For example, if by hand calculator the result for *c* above is 342" (seconds) and we wish to convert back into minutes, the answer will appear 5.7 (minutes). The .7 must then be multiplied by 60 to get the correct number of seconds, which in this case is 42". The correct answer for c then is 5'42" of arc.

### Example 1 (using a midnight ephemeris):

Before progressing to the next step in calculating a solar return chart, let us review an example - step by step - of finding a natal Sun to the nearest minute. Assume we have a young lady born November 1, 1969, at 9:48 AM, in Royal Oak, Michigan (Eastern Standard Time).

According to the outline above:

A. *Determine the Greenwich Mean Time (GMT) of birth:*

In this case, Eastern Standard Time (EST) is five hours prior to GMT. By adding five hours to the birth time it is determined that the *GMT of birth is 2:48 PM, November 1, 1969.* One should note that if the GMT of birth changes from a PM to an AM, that birthdate also moves forward by one day.

Determining the GMT of birth is very simple for those born in the continental U.S.A. For anyone born in the Eastern Standard Time Zone, add five hours; Central Standard Time Zone (CST), add six hours; Mountain Standard Time Zone (MST) add seven hours; and for Pacific Standard Time Zone (PST), add eight hours. One should also remember to correct for daylight savings or war time (subtract one hour). For countries east of GMT it is equally easy - just *subtract* from clock time the number of hours removed from GMT.

B. *Determine the hours and minutes that GMT of birth is removed from midnight of GMT birthdate. Reduce to total minutes.*

2:48 PM is 14 hours, 48 minutes after midnight. This is *888* minutes when reduced to total minutes (14 hours x 60 minutes = 840 minutes, plus 48 minutes = 888). This is *a* of proportion.

C. *Let b of proportion be 1440 minutes* - total number of minutes in a 24-hour day. No calculation is necessary here.

D. *Determine the daily motion of the Sun:*

1. By subtracting the midnight position of the Sun on the GMT birthdate, from midnight position of the Sun on day after GMT birthdate, the following is derived:

Sun, midnight GMT 11/2/69:  9°♏ 23' 54"
Sun, midnight GMT 11/1/69:  8°♏ 23' 54"
      Result:     =     1°    00' 00"

2. Reduce to total seconds:

      Result:     =     3600"

3. Let this (3600") be *d* of proportion.

E. *Determine the exact longitudinal position of the natal Sun:*

26

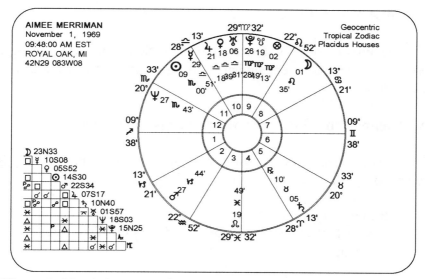

**Figure 3: Natal chart showing Sun position of native born November 1, 1969, 9:48 AM, Royal Oak, Mi.**

1. Use formula:

$$c = \frac{a \times d}{b}$$

so, $c = \dfrac{888 \times 3600}{1440} = \dfrac{3{,}196{,}800}{1440} = 2220"$ of arc

2. Convert result into minutes and seconds:
   $2220"/60' = 37'00"$

3. Add to midnight position of Sun's longitude on GMT birthdate:

| | |
|---|---|
| midnight on GMT birthdate: | 8°♏ 23' 54" |
| | + 37' 00" |
| natal Sun's exact longitude: | 9°♏ 00' 54" |

Thus her natal Sun is 9°♏ 00'54" of Scorpio.

## USING A NOON EPHEMERIS

The instructions for finding the natal Sun's longitude, using a *noon* ephemeris, are very similar to using a midnight ephemeris, and are as follows:

A. Determine the Greenwich Mean Time (GMT) of birth.

B. Determine how many hours and minutes this time (GMT) is removed from noon on the GMT date of birth.

    1. Reduce to *total minutes*.
    2. Note whether result is *before* or *after* noon. The result is *a* of proportion.

C. Let *b* of proportion be 1440 minutes, the number of minutes in a 24-hour day (60 x 24).

D. Determine the daily motion of the Sun:

    1. If GMT is *PM*, use noon position of the Sun on the GMT day of birth and day *after* birth.

    If GMT is *AM*, use noon positions of the Sun on GMT day of birth and day *before* birth.

    2. Subtract the lesser day position from the greater day position, using degrees, minutes, and *seconds* of each.

    3. Reduce the result to total *seconds*. Result will always be near 3600 seconds.

    4. Let this result be *d* of proportion.

E. Determine the exact longitudinal position of the natal Sun, using the following proportions:

28

$$\frac{a}{b} = \frac{c}{d}$$

wherein:

a = Total number of minutes GMT is removed from noon.

b = 1440 (total number of minutes in a day)

c = Distance the Sun has moved (or has yet to move) from noon position on GMT birthdate.

d = Daily motion of the Sun on the GMT birthdate.

1. *c*, the unknown is determined as follows:

$$c = \frac{a \times d}{b}$$

2. The result will be in *seconds* of solar arc. Covert back into minutes if the result is over 60 seconds.

3. Add (if GMT is PM) or subtract (if GMT is AM), to or from the noon position of the Sun on the GMT date of birth. This then is the longitude of the natal Sun, to the nearest degree, minute, and second of arc.

*Example 2, (using a noon ephemeris):*

Assume the client is born July 3, 1917, 10:26 AM, in New York City.

A. GMT is 10:26 AM + 5 hours = *3:26 PM.*

B. This is 3 hours, 26 minutes, *after* noon, or *206* total minutes. This is *a* of proportion.

C. There are *1440* total minutes in a day. This is *b* of proportion.

29

D. To determine the daily motion of the Sun, take the noon position of the Sun on the GMT birth date (7/3/17) and subtract from the noon position of the Sun on the day after the GMT birth (7/4/17).

Noon position 7/4/17:   11° ♋ 54' 32"
Noon position 7/3/17:   10° ♋ 57' 22"

Daily motion of Sun:          57' 10"

Reduced to total seconds, =     3430"
This is *d* of proportion.

E.  c = $\dfrac{a \times d}{b}$,  so c = $\dfrac{206 \times 3430}{1440}$   c = 490.68"

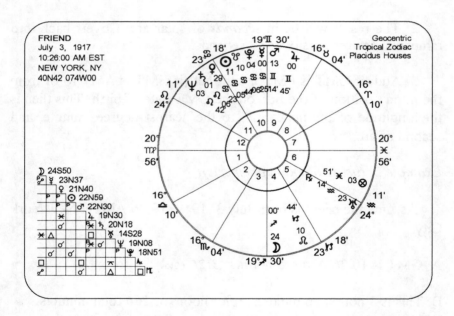

**Figure 4: Natal chart of native born July 3, 1917, 10:26 AM, in New York City, depicting exact position of natal Sun.**

Converting this result back into minutes and seconds - dividing by 60' (490.68"/60') - gives a result of 8.178', or, when converting

.178 minutes back into seconds, the final result is *08'11"* of solar arc. In other words, between noon and GMT (3:26 PM), the Sun (actually the Earth) moved 8' 11" of arc.

This result is then *added* (since GMT is PM) to the noon position of the Sun on the GMT birth date. Thus:

Noon position on 7/3/17　: 10° ♋ 57' 22"
+　　　　　　8' 11"
Exact position of natal Sun:　11° ♋ 05' 33"

## FINDING THE TIME OF THE SOLAR RETURN

The next step is to determine the exact time - the nearest minute - when the Sun returns to its precise natal position, for the year in which the solar return chart is desired. The method to determine this is as follows:

II. *Determining the time of the Solar Return* (using a midnight ephemeris):

A. Find the date in which the midnight position (GMT) of the transiting Sun is less than, but not greater than, the exact position of the natal Sun. The date should be within one day of the birthdate in most cases.

B. Subtract the position of the transiting Sun at midnight, GMT, from the position of the natal Sun.

　1. Reduce result to nearest *second* of arc.
　2. The result is $c$ of proportion.

C. Determine the daily motion of the transiting Sun.

　1. Subtract the position of the Sun at midnight of day which is *less than* natal Sun's longitude, from midnight position of Sun on the *day after* (which will be greater than natal Sun's longitude).

31

2. Reduce result to total seconds (which will be bear 3600").

3. The result will be *d* of proportion.

D. Determine the time of the solar return, GMT, using the same proportion as before, whereby:

a = Total number of minutes solar return is removed from midnight.
b = Total number of minutes in a 24-hour day, or 1440.
c = Distance the Sun has moved from midnight, GMT, to the exact longitude of the natal Sun's position.
d = Daily motion of the Sun on the solar return day.

1. *a* is now the unknown, and can be determined by the following formula:

$$a = \frac{b \times c}{d}$$

This will give the amount of time which has elapsed between midnight, GMT, and the actual solar return, thus making the time of the solar return easy to calculate.

2. The result will be in total minutes. Convert this result into hours and minutes of time, by dividing by 60 minutes.

3. Add this result to midnight. This, then, is the GMT of the solar return to the nearest minute (and even second, if one so wishes).

Let us now return to Example one, and illustrate the method of determining her solar return for 1976.

Example 1: Born November 1, 1969, 9:48 AM, Royal Oak, Michigan. Natal Sun's longitude is 9°♏ 00'54". We wish to determine the GMT of the solar return for 1976, same location.

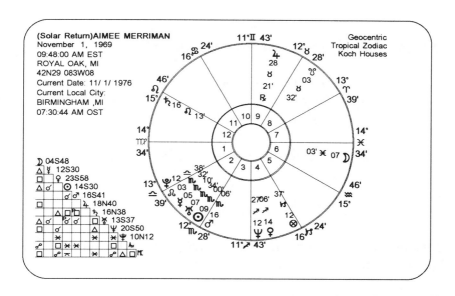

**Figure 5: Solar return for 1976 of native born November 1, 1969.**

A: *Find the date of the solar return*:

On November 1, 1976, the Sun at midnight, GMT, is 8°42'06" Scorpio. This is the closest date in which the transiting Sun is less than, but not greater than, the natal Sun.

B: *Subtract the position of the solar return (transiting) Sun as given at midnight, from natal Sun.* Reduce to total seconds of arc.

| Natal Sun 11/1/69: | 9°♏ 00' 54" |
|---|---|
| - Midnight Sun 11/1/76: | 8°♏ 42' 06" |
| | 18' 48" = 1128" |

C: *Daily motion of transiting Sun:*

$$11/2/76 = 9° \ 42' \ 06"$$
$$11/1/76 = 8° \ 42' \ 06"$$
$$1° \ 00' \ 00", \text{ or } 3600"$$

D: *Determine the time of the solar return, GMT*:

> b = 1440 minutes of time
> c = 1128 seconds of arc
> d = 3600 seconds of arc

1. if $a = \dfrac{b \times c}{d}$, then, $a = \dfrac{1440 \times 1128}{3600}$

> a = 451.2 minutes of time.

2. Converting this to hours and minutes: 451.2/60 minutes = 7.52 hours, or 7 hours, 31 minutes, 12 seconds.

Thus, GMT = 7:31.2 AM is the exact time of the solar return for 1976 (see Figure 5).

This, by the way, is the chart of the author's daughter. The solar return for 1976 represents the year she would acquire a step-mother as her father re-married after being divorced for three years.

Since repetition is an effective means of learning new (and somewhat complex) techniques, let's apply these steps to a second example.

Example 2: Client born July 3, 1917, 10:26 AM, in New York City. Natal Sun's longitude at birth is 11 05'33' Cancer. Again the objective is to determine the GMT of the solar return for 1976. She was located in Miami, Florida at that time. According to the instructions:

A: July 2, 1976, at midnight, GMT, the Sun is 10°♋ 14' 36". This is the closest date that is less than but not greater than the position of the natal Sun.

| B: | Natal Sun | 7/3/17: | 11° 05' 33" |
|---|---|---|---|
| - | Midnight Sun | 7/2/76: | 10° 14' 36" |
| | | | 50' 57" = 3057" |

This is how far the Sun (actually the Earth) moved from GMT midnight to the time of the solar return.

C: Daily motion of transiting Sun:

| | 7/3/76: | 11° 11' 48" |
|---|---|---|
| - | 7/2/76: | 10° 14' 36" |
| | | 57' 12" = 3432" |

D:     $a = \dfrac{b \times c}{d}$ where,     b = 1440 minutes
        c = 3057 seconds of arc
        d = 3432 seconds of arc

$a = \dfrac{1440 \times 3057}{3432}$ = 1282.6573 minutes of time

a = 21.38 hours, or 21 hours, 22 minutes, 48 seconds past midnight (21 hours, 22.8 minutes).

This result, then, corresponds to 9:22.8 PM, GMT, 7/2/76, as the exact moment of this person's solar return for 1976.

Once the exact time of the solar return has been determined through either the long-hand calculation method as just described, or through use of an accurate software program, the next step involves drawing up the horoscope for this time and place where the individual was located at that very moment. Again, this may done either by the long-hand method, or by the use of a software program that will do that for you (i.e. there are many fine "all-purpose" astrological programs present on the market today). But the question will arise: for which location? Many books state that the solar return should always be calculated according to the place of birth; others state that it should be calculated from the location where the individual will spend most of his or her time

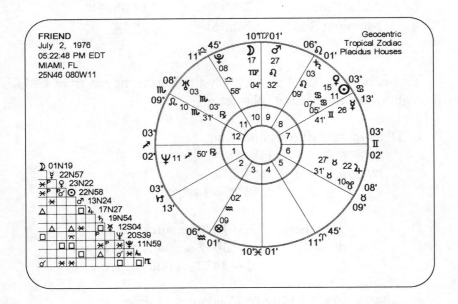

**Figure 6: Solar return for 1976 of native born July 3, 1917, 10:26 AM, in New York City, but present in Miami, Florida at time of 1976 solar return**

during the following year - such as one's residence. But for reasons stated in Chapter One, a solar return chart is most accurate when calculated from the exact place on Earth where the native was physically located at the time of the solar return (and preferably, the native will remain in the vicinity of that area for the following 24 hours).

The concept of location is extremely significant in studying the effect of solar returns for more reasons than those already mentioned. It brings into possibility the expression of self-determinism, or free-will, through the use of knowledge. If knowledge indeed is a pre-requisite to freedom (although in and of itself knowledge may hardly suffice), and if location at the time of the solar return is indeed a factor governing the "type" of horoscope that will apply to a certain cycle of time, then knowledge

36

of the solar return (astrology) combined with one's choice to be mobile means one can determine, to a certain extent, what kind of solar return chart one may have for any given year! It is true that one cannot control what relationship the planets will have to one another, or within the zodiac itself, at the time of a solar return. However one does  have a certain amount of control (through knowledge of astrology and especially of solar returns) as to what relationship the planets might have to the axes of the Earth. In other words, one can choose the angles and  houses of the horoscope one wishes to have in place for the next year.

Thus a solar return chart - and interpretation - is accurate only if 1) it is calculated to the exact degree, minute and second of arc of the natal Sun position, and 2) if it is calculated for the correct longitude and latitude of the individual's physical being at that exact moment of the solar return.

With these thoughts in mind, and with the correct chart, we can now begin the art of interpreting the solar return horoscope.

# 3 CHAPTER THREE

# INTERPRETATION: THE OVERALL "TONE" OF THE YEAR

The interpretation of any horoscope, including the solar return chart, is actually an art. It is the art of synthesizing, of taking symbols and their multi-combinations, and giving them meaning. That is why any work on interpretation can at best be only a guideline, showing what to look for, what principles to apply - when and where. Yet in the end, the beauty and accuracy (usefulness) of any horoscopic interpretation must depend upon the skill of the individual astrologer to synthesize a whole host of complex combination of symbols. This chapter will therefore serve as a guide to facilitate the astrologer's art of prediction.

The solar return chart need not be considered, or even used, separately from the natal chart. This has been one of the criticisms of the solar return chart - that it is used separately from the natal chart. Many astrologers believe they can derive sufficiently accurate interpretations through analyzing only the progressions and transits to the natal horoscope. It is true that transits and progressions yield very reliable interpretations, but the solar return chart need not be considered another type of chart altogether. This apparent dilemma is solved and the two systems are made compatible simply by inserting the natal planets and angles into and with the solar return horoscope. Progressions and transits still make the same aspects to the natal planets and angles, but they also make aspects to solar return planets and angles - but from the solar return houses instead of the natal ones. The result of interpreting transits and progressions in this manner is extremely accurate and insightful from the experience of this author.

Right now, however, we are concerned with interpreting the general conditions of the year signified by the solar return chart. The predictive part requires adequate preparation, and even the preparative material will be seen to be rather predictive in nature.

## GENERAL OVERVIEW FOR THE YEAR

At the time of one's solar return, planets are positioned throughout the sky in a division known as "houses." Houses are simply a 12-fold division of the sky as seen from a specific location upon Earth, like the location of one's solar return.

These 12 houses are furthermore categorized into three types: angular, succedent, and cadent houses. Each of these types has certain general meanings. The more planets one has in a certain type of house, the more it points to a certain "type" of year about to unfold. The character of the year will be shaped greatly by which house types have the most - and the least - number of planets.

In the analysis of the year ahead as signified by one's solar return, both the natal and the solar return planets are used according to where they fall within the *solar return horoscope* (and not the natal horoscope). If we count every planet - both natal and solar return - we get a sum of 20 (yes, count the Sun twice, one each for natal and solar return, even though they are in the same position). We then determine how many of these planets fall in angular (houses 1, 4, 7, and 10), succedent (houses 2, 5, 8, and 11), or cadent (houses 3, 6, 9, and 12) houses of the solar return chart. The sum must equal 20. Some readers may also wish to include the solar return house in which the natal ascendant falls, particularly if this inclusion breaks a tie. In this case, the total should equal 21.

## *HOUSE EMPHASIS*

**Majority Angular:** A potentially significant year will be shown by the presence of a majority of planets in the angular houses of one's solar return chart. These are the action houses, and if the majority of planets fall here, and moreso if cardinal signs also appear on the solar return angles, it indicates a year of much activity. Furthermore it is likely to be a year in which one begins many new projects. New relationships are likely to commence and the year is likely to be one in which the native will receive much attention - especially if the Sun or Moon are posited in an angular house as well. In short, this promises to be an eventful year, a year of great importance in one's lifetime.

At best, it signifies adventure and new beginnings with great excitement. At worse, it may indicate unwanted or unflattering attention, and difficulties (fights) in relationships, or disputes at work. It may also indicate an egotistic craving for attention that turns others away. Thus careful attention should be placed upon significant relationships this year. Insensitivity to the cares of others may lead to separations.

**Majority Succedent**: The majority of planets falling in the succedent houses of the solar return chart signifies the completion of projects already underway at the time of the solar return, especially so if fixed signs are also on any angle. Conditions may be entered into that are difficult to change, or even terminate. One may anticipate a year of many responsibilities with the resultant effect being one of great character-maturity development. Values are likely to become stronger, one's principles become more firm, which could be a positive in the future. In addition, one's goals in life may become more established, which could ultimately lead to future success.

In short, this is not likely to be a year of change - at least not voluntarily. It may favor finishing - or at least continuation of - tasks already in process at the beginning of this solar return period.

At its best, one may have a sense of security and stability, and possibly completion. At its worst, the year may be characterized with boredom, frustration, and lack of challenge or inspiration. Resistance to change, to try new things, or to get cooperation from others may also be noted. It may also indicate a tendency to stay with something (or someone) too long, past the point of satisfying returns. This may be due to too much "pride", which may result in further loss of face due to one's refusal to "cut losses short", or refusal to give up something of an obsession when it is apparent (to everyone else) that it is not going to get any better. Too much pride and not enough flexibility may create problems in relationships. On the other hand, tenacity and loyalty may be what saves significant relationships from failing this year

**Majority Cadent**: A solar return chart showing a majority of planets in the cadent houses suggests a year of flux as far one's affairs in the world are concerned. This is moreso the case if the chart also has mutable signs on any angle. It may also indicate a year of mental activity and preparation for something in one's future (beyond the current year). One may end up viewing this as a year of training, apprenticeship, or some sort of preparation for another phase soon to appear in life. Many plans will likely change, and the native might not feel so much in control as usual, but if adaptable (and conditions will be such that this is advised), then many favorable alternatives to the current approach in life will arise.

If, on the other hand, one is not adaptable, then this situation generally indicates a year of irritation and frustration. All significant affairs entered into seem to be with others who are uncooperative, or with unstable situations over which there is little control. Unless one wishes to work on special mental projects, a majority of planets posited in the solar return cadent houses is not the most favorable condition. All cadent houses are the twelfth house of the angular house which follows. Hence an overriding majority of planets here can suggest the undoing of former and current efforts (shown by angular houses). With this set-up (unless there is some sort of balance shown elsewhere, or else a writing project is

41

contemplated), one might seriously consider traveling elsewhere for the solar return event - somewhere that will move the majority of planets out of the cadent houses, and perhaps into angular houses (i.e. westward). It is best to consult with a trained and qualified professional Astrologer for assistance in this matter. If unable to travel, then it is advisable to make time available for meditation or daily contemplation during this year, for the tendency towards restlessness and lack of focus may be greater than usual. Meditation can be the antidote for that.

At best, the majority of planets in cadent houses favors writing, teaching, and traveling ventures. It could indicate favorable legal matters, depending upon which planets are in or rule the ninth house. It may also indicate many experiences of inspiration, and even moments of a joyful outpouring, of bliss (compassion) for others. It could be a time of great spiritual awareness. At worst, it suggests a great desire for change, but no real change is effected. It is thus a potentially restless period in which one's direction in life is not very clear. It may also correlate to illness, possibly induced by psychological stress. One is advised to watch diet very carefully, and stay with an exercise program.

**Balance**: A balance would be achieved with the presence of at least three, and preferably four or more planets in each house type. Having a balance of planets in each house type is most favorable. This indicates a "balanced" approach to life, a nice combination of initiative, follow-through, and inspiration or new ideas.

# 4. CHAPTER FOUR

# THE HOUSE CONTAINING THE SUN

The Sun is definitely the most important planet (star) to consider in the interpretation of solar returns, for the whole chart is based upon its principle. It is the only placement which is always identical (by longitude) in the natal as well as the solar return chart. Its house position shows where the greatest growth may take place during the year and where one may express the self creatively. It also denotes the area of greatest recognition as well as the area where the individual will "identify" the self this year. It is an indication of success according to house placement - an area where the person may "shine" and show honor, a place where one may take pride in his or her accomplishments.

The houses have basically the same principles in the interpretation of a solar return chart as they do in a natal chart. The only difference is that the solar return houses are temporal in nature, and thus the actual interpretation of their meaning must be slightly modified because of this factor. In other words, the interpretation is for one year only, and not as a life-long condition.

## HOUSE POSITION OF SUN

The following represent tendencies for the year, given the placement of the Sun in any given solar return chart.

**1st house**: There is a tendency to project a very confident and vibrant self-image for the coming year. One's efforts tend to be successful and bring much recognition and attention. One may come across with radiance and happiness to others, with a sense of strength and "take charge". One may assume positions of leadership and control, and be the one "in charge" in his/her surroundings. Overall it portends good health and psychological strength, and a year of great personal growth.

It may also indicate financial fears. Even though there is much activity, there may be some question as to ability to save or accumulate wealth. The "I desire" or "I am" part of the self at this time may be quite strong too, and one must be careful of appearing too egotistical, self-centered, or demanding of others.

**2nd house**: Great emphasis is placed upon values, and how one attracts and deals with financial matters. The results, often financial, of one's efforts prior to this time tend to reap success this year. If the native has been working on a project prior to the time of this solar return, then this year may bring into fruition the completion and success of that project. It may indicate very creative financial ideas - new ways to increase profit or income. In fact, one's attention may be heavily focused on money, income, or profit - for better or worse. If focused purely upon money, then a quality of "greed" and/or "possessiveness" may be noticed unfavorably by others. The native may also come into possession of valuable goods. Overall, it favors growth in income, savings, and security, particularly if in trine to the solar return Midheaven.

**3rd house:** Great growth may take place in intellectual and mental pursuits. Very creative ideas may lead one to engage successfully in writing, speaking, or sales. This year may be favorable for marketing ideas, or writing projects. It also indicates a year that may highlight relationships with neighbors, brothers, and/or sisters, and/or correspondence with others (i.e. short journeys, letter writing, telephone calls, etc.). Furthermore it can indicate a year in which one purchases a new automobile, or some durable

44

communications goods (i.e. computer), that enhances work efficiency. Overall, the native is apt to identify him/herself in terms of their ideas, and their success in relating those ideas determines the degree of their self-confidence for the year.

This placement might also indicate domestic problems, maladies involving members of one's family or apprehensions of such. A tendency towards worry may be overcome through creative mental pursuits, like writing, or studying something of interest.

**4th house**: Great personal growth may be experienced in regards to home, family, parents and/or spiritual direction (the "ultimate" home). The native may now come into contact with his/her "true self, "one's most inner nature and basic needs. This year may provide a very personal and very deep understanding of one's very essence. In family matters and all types of domestic concerns, the native is the one who may have the expertise. Here one is confident and tends to exhibit fine qualities of leadership. One's role in the family is central this year, and in this realm the native may shine. One may become the "hero," and thus receive great attention from those who are closest to him/her. The native may identify closely with their role and successes in the family or home environment. One may be placed in the role of the "benevolent parent", or if the native is a child, they may bring great honor to the family.

However, there may also be fears involving one's children and/or lovers. There may be fears associated with taking specific risks. One may be more comfortable not taking risks this year, except perhaps in real estate matters, which could turn out very successful.

**5th house**: There is great potential for creativity, fun, and happiness this year. Romance, entertainment, self-expressive creative pursuits, and conditions involving one's children (or younger people) are favorably highlighted. This year may deal more with "new" loves rather than "old" loves. The native may be the center of much attention and adoration, particularly if the Sun trines the Ascendant. It is a year favoring great creative self-expression,

45

and one in which risks seem to pay off. If the native has children, either they "shine", or the native "shines" in the eyes of their children. There is much to be proud of here. In financial matters, speculative strategies may be favorable. It certainly favors a year of entertainment, so one is encouraged to attend many parties, and even host a few.

However, excessive amounts of self-indulgent activities and "running about" may be detrimental to one's health, and hence a certain amount of self-restraint is advised. Fears involving work, or "quality" of one's work, might also be present at occasional intervals.

**6th house**: Great growth or improvement may take place in regards to one's health and work matters. Service given to or received from others is also highly appreciated. The solar return year emphasizes the nature of one's work - the craftsmanship involved in it (if any) and the value of one's creative expressions. One tends to be very creative in applying a particular craft or skill, should the native possess one. Much recognition for one's talent may come if indeed there is a talent, particularly if the Sun trines the Midheaven. This is a year in which one can enjoy great personal satisfaction from work, assuming work has a creative challenge to it.

If one's work is not personally meaningful, then creative means of escape from it may be sought. This is a year in which one craves to identify with his/her work, and if this effort is unsuccessful, then instead of good health, the native may experience a series of ailments that are related to job stress. During the year one may also experience fears concerning marriage and/or partnerships and the possibility of deception through partners. If partnerships are very important and the native is currently encountering stress in partnerships, then he/she may wish to consider traveling for the solar return, and thus move the Sun to the 5th or 7th house. One is advised to consult a well-trained, professional Astrologer for assistance.

**7th house**: One is likely to identify in terms of marriage (or thoughts of it), partnerships, legal matters, and popularity with others this year. It is a very active year with others - especially others with whom there is a significant relationship. There may be an emphasis upon who represents the native in public - and how that person represents the native (agent, lawyer, manager, spouse, etc.). There are quite possibly many new and advantageous unions entered into, such as marriage if one is unmarried prior to this birthday. This year favors socializing, as it portends great social upswing in one's status among others. If one is married, this can indicate a year of great success and recognition for the partner, or for both the native and the spouse (partner) as a team.

However one must be careful of seeking status too gregariously. A tendency to lose one's identity - or to "sell out" one's own principles - in order to be accepted by others, may be a real danger this year. Accusations of being a "social climber" can sting.

**8th house**: The greatest growth this year may come from experiences with other people's psychological values and monies (i.e. gifts, insurance, grants, scholarships, loans, etc.). Matters involving death and consequent estate settlements may be highlighted. So too may long-term investments and research projects requiring much investigation into "hidden" or "unknown" matters. In fact, one's identity may be strengthened considerably if involved in some research project. The completion of that project may bring great recognition or reward. In the course of conducting research or investigation, one may become quite excited with findings. It may be quite a "discovery" process, and in so doing, several opportunities and choices may open for the native. In addition, this year may place great emphasis (favorable) upon the financial outlook of one's partner, especially if the Sun favorably aspects the Midheaven.

However the year may also portend an ending to love or romantic affairs. Thus it could indicate a change in one's social nature, which is usually precipitated by some outward crisis between work (duty) and relationships (love), particularly if the Sun is located very close to the midpoint of the third quadrant. The year may highlight sexual matters and areas in one's life which may now be transformed - endings and starting over again. This is not an ideal position to find one's solar return Sun. One would be encouraged to travel somewhere for the solar return, placing the Sun in either the 7th or 9th houses nearby. Consult a well-trained, qualified professional Astrologer for assistance.

**9th house**: Great personal growth and satisfying personal experiences are now possible in regards to education, law, dealings with foreign peoples, philosophy, and long (foreign) travel. This is a year that favors preparation for something significant in the near future (with much anticipation and/or excitement), as in education or training, for something greater in life, that may actually evolve the next year. All matters tend to go well that deal with publishing, foreign affairs, or with those who are of a different nationality than the native. It furthermore favors second marriages (should it apply) and court decisions. If the Sun is trine to the Ascendant, then one is likely to feel exuberance, happiness, and a general sense of growth this year.

However, there may very well be fears and perhaps even free-floating anxiety concerning one's vocation or life direction in a mundane sense. Keep in mind that this is a year of training and preparation, and these fears will likely give way to more concrete and positive developments after this year.

**10th house**: Much success and great growth are highlighted in regards to one's career and professional status (even social status as the former enhances the latter). One may now identify closely - and favorably - with one's vocation and standing in the community. This is a period highlighting accomplishment and the rewards that go with it - both financially and socially. Much recognition and praise may come to the native as a result of these successes. The year may also favor relationships with one's father, employer, supervisor, or superior of any kind. In a sense, one now becomes a person of destiny because of one's nature to set up and pursue goals, and furthermore to accomplish them within the forthcoming year. There may be a sense of one's "work to do" during this year, as in a spiritual sense.

However, this position could also indicate disappointments and apprehensions concerning one's friends. Perhaps they are not happy with perceived changes in the native. The fact that these successes are relatively new means that one may even experience fears of failure, which may seem strange since it is at a time when one is in fact likely to be doing so well. There may be insecurity in regards to emotions and feelings, although one's efforts may now be designed to achieve more security and do away with such unrealistic and negative illusions.

**11th house**: This year highlights professional or career rewards and accomplishments; the realization of one's vocational efforts. It also highlights friends and successful conditions existing with them that interest the native. Much personal growth is possible as a result of contacts and experiences with groups activities, especially when involving a position of leadership and powerful influence on the part of the native. One may identify closely with the realization of many personal hopes and wishes this year.

However, if the Sun is near the midpoint of the 4th quadrant, it may signify a year in which one's authority is seriously challenged. A power play may emerge in a group setting. One's motivations and dedication to the "cause" may be questioned (as opposed to being in it "for the personal glory"). One may be forced to examine his/her own intentions, and this may actually end up having a positive result. Regarding the power play... the native wins.

**12th house:** During this year, one may identify closely with efforts behind the scenes, or out of the public's eye. The year favors charity and volunteer work. It may also favor rest, relaxation and seclusion, as it may signify a withdrawing phase of one's life. It may be beneficial for work with institutions, or even psychic development and meditative pursuits. It favors research and doing activities by oneself, and out of the limelight.

However, experiences of vague apprehensiveness and self-doubt may be encountered. If planets herein are not favorable by aspect and one fails to utilize proper care, then it may indicate hospitalization, imprisonment or confinement of some kind. This is not the most desirable house to find a majority of solar return planets, or the Sun, unless the favorable goals listed above are of great value to the native at the moment. It may be advisable to travel somewhere for this solar return, trying to place the Sun in either the first or eleventh house. Consult a well-trained and qualified professional Astrologer to assist.

# 5. CHAPTER FIVE

# WHERE THE ACTION IS: HOUSE CONTAINMENT AND CUSP CONJUNCTIONS OF PLANETS TO THE SOLAR RETURN CHART

A specific area of life is highly emphasized for the year of the solar return if a solar return or natal planet *conjuncts any house cusp*. The orb of the conjunction in which this is most evident is approximately 3 degrees, 45 minutes, either side of the house cusp. The house system preferred by the author is Placidus, Tropical method.

The planet making the conjunction describes the *nature of activities* - events, conditions - that tend to unfold in the coming year. This planet's nature is highlighted as being prominent for this year if conjunct a house cusp. These activities, denoted by the planet, will tend to take place in *specific areas of life*, as indicated by the house cusp involved. These areas of life signified by the house cusp being conjunct will thus be specially highlighted during the next year.

To get a glimpse of which activities and which areas of life are being highlighted in this manner, it is necessary to combine the *planetary meanings* with the *house meanings* that apply (the specific planets conjunct the specific house cusps). Although the following descriptions apply most strongly to those planets that conjunct a house cusp, the interpretations will also be valid to a lesser extent to any given planet in any given solar return house. In the following section, it is furthermore advisable to read both the natal and solar return planets as they fall within the solar return chart, with slightly more emphasis placed upon solar return ones.

**The Sun:** Whatever solar return house contains the Sun is the area which holds the greatest growth possibilities during the next year. It signifies recognition and attention in matters to do with this area of life signified by that house. This is an area where one may express great creativity and leadership skills. It signifies an area where one will likely identify him/herself in the next year, and with motivation and effort will likely succeed. The native may exhibit qualities that are radiant, energetic, confident, and show leadership potential in this area of life. However one may also impress others as being arrogant in this same area.

For a specific interpretation of the Sun conjunct a certain house cusp, review the previous chapter ("House Containing The Sun"). Even though that chapter dealt with the Sun in a given house, it will also apply (even in greater measure) if the Sun is within 3 degrees, 45 minutes of a given house cusp.

**The Moon**: Look to the solar return houses that the native's natal and solar return Moon fall, giving special emphasis if either is conjunct a solar return house cusp. These houses denote where many changes - and hence, events - may occur during this year. These are areas where one may have great needs, especially emotionally. One's public image for the year may be effected by circumstances which unfold in this area of life. It also indicates areas of life in which one may form significant relationships (intimate ones) for the year. It can indicate a potential partnership (or marriage) in that area of life. It may also indicate where dependencies with other people may form, and these dependencies may not be healthy for the native unless a high degree of trust is present. Personal qualities that may be exhibited in these areas of life include sensitivity, caring, emotionalism, but also fickleness, restlessness, and defensiveness (resistance and/or denial).

**Mercury:** Look to the solar return houses that the native's natal and solar return Mercury fall, giving special emphasis if either is conjunct a solar return house cusp. This denotes areas of life in which correspondence, writings, trading, business deals and transactions, signing of papers, and intellectual interests may lie for the year. It describes areas of life in which one may negotiate deals. It represents potential areas of commerce, of buying and selling. New ideas may be expressed or learned here. In addition, one may be of service to others in these same areas of life. It is in these areas wherein one may be called forth to deal with younger people. In short, this is where a great deal of one's mental energy may be spent in the next year, and where communications skills can be a great asset. It presents ample opportunities for learning. The personal qualities that may be exhibited in these areas are intelligence, business acumen, knowledge, communication (but perhaps critical) skills, and sales or persuasive (as in logical argument) abilities.

**Venus:** Look to the solar return houses that the native's natal and solar return Venus fall, giving special emphasis if either is conjunct a solar return house cusp. Relationships, love matters, romantic interests, compatibility and harmony with others are all highlighted in these areas of life. It shows where one may experience personal popularity, as well as potentially favorable developments in finances, valuables, and possessions. It denotes where the native may exhibit good taste - or style - for the current year. It shows where one may be seen as being attractive and thus find compatibility. It shows where one may acquire something of value. It also denotes areas in which others are likely to show favor to the native. It may be that one finds things which are pleasing to his/her nature, i.e. an aesthetic sense of beauty. It may indicate areas wherein artistic and creative types are met. More significantly it will show where one may make valuable contacts - and it describes the types of contacts - which one may use later on. The personal qualities one tends to exhibit in these areas of life include graciousness, diplomacy, sociability, mediation, but also perhaps, jealousy, indecisiveness, and possessiveness.

53

**Mars:** Look to the solar return houses that the native's natal and solar return Mars fall, giving special emphasis if either is conjunct a solar return house cusp. These are areas of life wherein one is likely to initiate new ventures. Here one may initiate a pioneering spirit and eagerness to try new things, and if favorably placed and aspected, success is very possible; if afflicted, then one must guard against an over-impulsive nature which could lead to failure of pursuits. This is an area of great motivation and activity - an arena of "action." It also denotes where one tends to be competitive, or meets with competition from others. Furthermore, this shows where the native is likely to experience discordance with others, and possibly engage in quarrels or disputes. It may be wise to utilize great caution and self-control in these areas and relationships ruled by these houses, as one can be over-impulsive and rash. The personal qualities exhibited in these area are assertiveness, competitiveness, appearing to be driven, but perhaps also argumentative and pushy.

**Jupiter:** Look to the solar return houses that the native's natal and solar return Jupiter fall, giving special emphasis if either is conjunct a solar return house cusp. These denote areas where unions and matters of "good fortune" may occur; the areas where one might succeed and expand in a favorable way. Beneficial contacts and opportunities are likely to arise, so it is to the native's advantage to push matters (i.e. be assertive perhaps) in these areas. One will tend to meet with favor from other people here, particularly on a social level. It also portends areas in which educational and teaching opportunities may be presented. In short, look for success and happiness in these areas over the next year. However, also be aware of a tendency to "over-indulge" here too. Temptations to go against one's basic principles of integrity may be strong, so one must use common sense and good judgment in order to enjoy these areas to their maximum potential - without debilitating consequences later on. The personal qualities one tends to exhibit in these areas include friendliness, hopefulness, optimism, happiness, and generosity, but also perhaps indulgence, exaggeration, and the appearance of being "too loose."

54

**Saturn:** Look to the solar return houses that the native's natal and solar return Saturn fall, giving special emphasis if either is conjunct a solar return house cusp. This signifies areas in which one is likely to experience many (perhaps too many) obligations and commitments to others; areas of great responsibility, demands, and consequent seriousness. Much work, self-discipline and control are required in matters signified by these houses, and without proper attention, these matters could very well prove to be burdensome and the cause of delays and personal disappointments. If handled properly, then one may establish the foundations of a long-term cycle. It can also represent the beginning of a long, beneficial relationship in these areas of one's life. But if patience, self-control and discipline are not exercised here, then much frustration may be encountered due to setbacks and delays in the realization of goals. Furthermore, friendships may prove to be burdensome rather than helpful in pursuits involving these areas of life. It is also possible that matters from the past come back into one's life now. Dealings with older people and those in positions of authority, and activities involving government or law enforcement agencies could arise if they pertain to these areas of life. One must remember to be totally accountable in matters to do with these houses. There are no magical qualities about the conditions ruled by this set up. These areas are reality, and as such, may represent loses or setbacks if not handled responsibly. The personal qualities one tends to exhibit in these house areas include seriousness, studiousness, goal-oriented, responsible, but perhaps also pessimistic, critical, and judgmental, even depressive.

**Uranus:** Look to the solar return houses that the native's natal and solar return Uranus fall, giving special emphasis if either is conjunct a solar return house cusp. These are areas where sudden changes are to be experienced, where matters are apt to be rather erratic and unpredictable during the year. It shows where one may either encounter separations from established relationships or attractions to new ones. It indicates an area where ingenuity may be applied, or an "awakening" transpires, frequently attracting others to the native because of such "original" ideas. It is possible that new developments in technology or with computers and/or software programs play an important role for the native in these areas during the year. It signifies areas of life where one might become extraordinary, or at the least, non-conforming and unconventional. Here one may expect the unexpected to occur. That which is taken for granted as secure, isn't; that which was never expected to work out, may indeed work out. Surprises are in store for the native here, so it is best to be flexible and adaptable in. It could be exciting or disturbing. It is also an area where one may exhibit a very poor sense of timing - he/she is ahead of oneself and others. The personal qualities one tends to exhibit are charisma, excitability, inventiveness, ingenuousness, but also a tendency towards arrogance, rebelliousness, and over-zealousness.

**Neptune**: Look to the solar return houses that the native's natal and solar return Neptune fall, giving special emphasis if either is conjunct a solar return house cusp. These are areas where one is likely to be idealistic, imaginative, given to fantasies and illusions and infatuations, but at the same time aesthetical expressions. One tends to be vulnerable and even gullible during the current year in these areas, at least in matters of the mundane world. The native might be easily tricked, deceived or even betrayed. Hence, he/she is advised to exercise discrimination and discernment and to not harbor false illusions and hopes in these areas. At the same time wonderful, pleasurable, romantic, and dream-like circumstances may arise in these same areas. Music, creativity, and imaginative ideas may play important roles in these areas now. In addition, the native may have a "romantic mind", or romantic experiences here. It is an area where one may be of wonderful help to others, such as in a counseling capacity. But it is also a realm in which misunderstandings may arise, oftentimes due to mis-information or mis-diagnosis, so one must make certain that facts are correct. The personal qualities one tends to exhibit here include compassion, sensitivity, romance, idealism, but perhaps also confusion, nebulousness, and ambiguity.

**Pluto:** Look to the solar return houses that the native's natal and solar return Pluto fall, giving special emphasis if either is conjunct a solar return house cusp. These represent areas in which the native may experience potential greatness and/or may influence others with considerable power. It also represents areas in which things, matters, and people may be eliminated, removed, terminated, or at least transformed. These are areas that may require many reforms and major changes within one's life flow. In addition these areas may describe one's relationship to, or position within, groups. It may describe one's relationship to other people's assets and values. Oftentimes, something "dies" here, something is taken from the life here, or at least threatened with termination or removal in some way. A healing may be necessary in one of these areas of life during the course of the year in question. The personal qualities one tends to exhibit are intensity, depth, profundity, and power, but perhaps also obsessive and coercive qualities pertaining to these areas of life.

**The Natal Ascendant:** Look to the solar return house cusp (or house) that contains the natal Ascendant. This house cusp signifies a special area of importance to the native this year. He/she is likely to project much energy into this area. Immediate attention may be necessary to handle circumstances which arise in this area. It is an area in which one hopes to succeed (and probably will), to "look good," both to oneself and to others.

**Natal Midheaven**: Look to the solar return house cusp (or house) that contains the natal Midheaven. This is an area where one may accomplish great tasks. It is a special area wherein lies a sense of personal destiny and unfoldment during the forthcoming year, an area of great expectation, where a great degree of professionalism may be both developed and expressed. It is an area in which one may have to deal with superiors, but if adequately prepared, then rewards may result. There is a sense of challenge, and "work to be done" in this area.

**Natal Descendant:** Look to the solar return house cusp (or house) that contains the natal Descendant. This is an area in which the native may co-merge with others, where one may find and form partnerships. In this area one may feel a special sense of "relation to" others. Here one may attract others as a result of what he/she projects to the world. It describes the nature of what one attracts, both in terms of people and events (each are symbolic in astrology of lessons to be learnt). This is also an area requiring one to "cope with" circumstances, perhaps arising out of his/her control.

**Natal Nadir:** Look to the solar return house cusp (or house) that contains the natal Nadir. This is an area of importance to one's family and domestic concerns. It may also be an area in which one gains a glimpse of his/her inner self at work during the year, and thereby come to an understanding of his/her basic essence. In these areas, one might feel, and find, one's "roots," or deepest and most personal sense of identity and/or security. This is the area which most likely links the soul to the conscious mind during the current year, wherein one may now begin to find new answers concerning the nature of his/her own personal reality (and does not depend upon others to define it). It signifies where the native may discover his/her needs, in contrast to one's desires.

We have just outlined the specific activities, conditions, and personal qualities of the planets that are emphasized during a given solar return year, particularly if they conjunct a house cusp. Now we must combine those meanings with the particular house cusp meanings, in order to derive an understanding as to which areas of life are effected by these activities, conditions, and personal qualities. Therefore take the meanings of the planets given above, and apply them to the delineation of the houses given below, with special emphasis given to any natal or solar return planet that conjuncts a solar return house cusp.

**1st house (Ascendant):** Any natal or solar return planet conjunct the Ascendant pertains to the overall quality or character of one's efforts for the year. It describes the manner in which one comes across to others; one's immediate surroundings, and how one tends to conduct oneself, or present oneself to others. This deals with one's health, one's basic energy level, and in general, how one sees the current year - the "umbrella" of the year, the predominant "attitude". It describes what one desires of oneself and for oneself this year. As an example, if Saturn (natal or solar return) conjuncts the solar return ascendant, then the native is likely to be more serious and worried, perhaps expecting the worst throughout the year. On the other hand, if Jupiter conjuncts the ascendant, then the native is likely to be more jovial, optimistic, hopeful, and expect the best throughout the year.

**2nd house:** This is very simple. It pertains to the native's money, income, savings, and new possessions. For instance, if natal or solar return Saturn conjuncts this house cusp, the individual will tend to worry about money and perhaps even suffer a financial loss during the year (depends upon aspects to Saturn). There may be a loss of income. However if Jupiter conjuncts this cusp, then there may be great optimism about money and income. Perhaps there is a pay raise, or the sale of something for great profit.

**3rd house:** This pertains to one's mental state and intellectual endeavors; communications; automobiles and computers - or anything that assists in communications; neighbors, brothers and sisters; writings and correspondence. As an example, solar return or natal Venus conjunct the solar return third house may indicate a year in which one places great value on knowledge or learning. Perhaps one is offered a contract (agreement) for a writing project, or a sales position. It may also indicate favorable events for one's sister or female neighbor. One may come into possession of a valuable book or idea. If Mars is there, however, one may be given towards many disputes. One may also be extremely motivated to write or initiate sales in business. It may highlight one's brothers, or male neighbors.

**4th house (I.C.):** This pertains to one's home and family; also one's basic needs, the inner self, the "real you." This house describes one's domestic setting, the people one lives with, and one's parents. It may bring to importance matters dealing with real estate. For instance, if one wishes to sell or buy a home this year, it may be quite favorable to find natal or solar return Sun, Jupiter, or Mercury posited in conjunction to the I.C. Finding Saturn or Pluto here however may not result in the sale or purchase of a home as hoped for, at least not without difficulties along the way (i.e. delays or even rejections).

**5th house:** This pertains to one's lovers, children, and the people one socializes with (i.e. parties with). It also has to do with speculative ventures and pursuits of fun and entertainment. It rules creative pursuits, but mostly has to do with one's capacity to enjoy life and relationships with children. For instance, placing the natal or solar return Sun, Venus, Jupiter, Uranus or Neptune may indicate a year of wonderful and exciting romances. Placing the Moon there may result in a serious and long-term relationship, perhaps eventually resulting in marriage, especially if trine to the solar return Ascendant or Midheaven. If one is already married, each of these placements can represent favorable developments with children, or travel to places of great pleasure.

**6th house**: This pertains to one's health and/or work setting. Regarding work, it deals with "how" one works and with "whom" one works. For example, finding solar return or natal Mercury placed on this cusp can indicate a very busy work year, one which requires much intelligence and decision-making. However if Uranus or Saturn are posited here, one might encounter unexpected problems at work and with certain work relations. It could also indicate health problems, perhaps serious if Saturn is involved in other afflictions, like to the ascendant ruler.

**7th house (Descendant):** This pertains to the native's marriage and/or partnerships (including business); it also pertains to others who represent or misrepresent the native (lawyers, spokespersons, open enemies). As an example, Saturn, Pluto or Neptune located on the solar return descendant can suggest enemies and trouble with people who are deceptive and untrustworthy, perhaps even threatening. It may portend difficulties in one's marriage, or personal problems with one's spouse. However, finding the Sun, Moon, Venus or Jupiter there could indicate great happiness and positive developments in regards to one's partnerships and/or marriage. If not married, it is a good indication of becoming married during the year (or at least attending a special wedding).

**8th house:** This pertains to one's dealings with taxes, insurance matters, estate and death matters. It also pertains to sexual matters and concerns. It may describe the nature of threats one encounters during the year, but if positive, may also describe gifts, loans, scholarships, grants, etc. It describes the nature of one's research or investigative pursuits. It may also indicate conflicts between obligations to others versus work which one wishes to pursue. As an example of how it pertains to sexual concerns, finding one's natal or solar return Saturn conjunct the solar return 8th house cusp can indicate temporary impotency in a man or lack of interest in sexual matters altogether in a woman. It can also indicate an audit of one's finances, perhaps by the IRS (in the United States). Finding Mars or Venus conjunct the 8th house cusp on the other hand can indicate a renewed passion and sexual interest in either a man or a woman.

**9th house:** This pertains to one's long distance travels, legal decisions, publishing, educational pursuits, as well as in-laws and second marriage concerns if they apply. It also deals with philosophical matters, like religion and "the meaning life". Placing one's natal or solar return Jupiter or Mercury on the cusp of the solar return ninth house can indicate a year of notable travel (perhaps to foreign lands), education, or legal experiences. It is favorable for a court decision in one's favor, and also for the publishing of a book if one is so inclined.

**10th house (Midheaven):** This house cusp pertains to one's career and vocation; one's status in the community; one's accomplishments; one's role as the head of the company, enterprise, or household; the father-figures in one's life (father, employer, supervisor). Planets located here suggest a peak experience in one's life according to the nature of the planet (Venus would be love; Sun recognition/fame; Jupiter travel, education, or publishing venture; Mercury a business deal or mental effort; Saturn perhaps a major disappointment or loss, even death of a significant person; Moon a family or real estate venture; Neptune may relate to a scandal, etc.). Having a natal or solar return benefic (Sun, Venus or Jupiter) conjunct the solar return Midheaven is - by itself - a very favorable configuration. It is usually favorable to travel at the time of one's solar return to a location that would provide this setup, if possible.

**11th house:** This pertains to one's friends, as well as people with whom the native may have "power struggles"; it describes one's professional rewards and accomplishments; the realization of one's efforts; dealings within groups. For instance, if one had the Sun or Jupiter posited on the cusp of the solar return 11th house, then one might expect successful dealings with groups. It would be favorable to be the leader of a group during this year. Having Mars, Saturn or Pluto on the cusp, though, might indicate great power struggles within group settings, and challenge to the native's authority.

**12th house:** This pertains to one's dealings behind the scenes, or the behind-the-scenes-dealings which effect the native; hospitals, prisons, jails, places of confinement; one's "fantasy" world; places of reclusion; one's secrets and private world. Having a planet conjunct this house cusp is generally not a favorable arrangement. It could obscure the benefits of the planet, while at the same time magnify its negative features. For instance, finding Jupiter conjunct the 12th house cusp might negate the positive and optimistic attitudes associated with Jupiter, while at the same time indicate an exaggeration of unfounded fears and phobias. On a positive note, it might indicate great sacrifice for the benefit of another which is very much appreciated. The native may feel heartfelt thanks from others for his/her help. It could also indicate socializing with people of past confinement (i.e. criminals?). Furthermore it may indicate some amount of luck in matters of potential confinement (doesn't go to jail because of a legal technicality in native's favor).

# 6. CHAPTER SIX

## PERCEIVING REALITY AND RELATIONSHIPS: PLANETS IN ASPECT TO THE SOLAR RETURN HORIZON

Since the time and location of the solar return set up a structure (astrologically) for which an experience (the forthcoming year) will occur, the foundation of that structure becomes extremely significant. This structural foundation is symbolized by the angles of the horoscope, the axes of the Earth, in which all the zodiac and all of the planets combine within. The relationship of these axes (angles) to the planets - both natal and solar return planets - gives special meaning to the structure of experience the native will undergo during the period of the solar return's influence (one year).

A planet (solar return and natal) in close aspect to the solar return horizon (Ascendant-Descendant) - orb no more than seven degrees - affects the nature of how one perceives reality, how one projects the self, what one considers important in dealing with others, and the dominant behavior as well as activities which one expresses in the world during the year. It also describes how one tends to handle situations as they arise.

The following represents a brief description of the planets (solar return and natal) in close aspect (i.e. less than seven degrees) to the Ascendant/Descendant axis in the solar return wheel. A plus (+) sign refers to a trine, sextile and certain conjunction (i.e. involving benefics and neutrals) aspects; a minus (-) sign refers to the square and some conjunction (i.e. involving malefics) aspects. There are no oppositions because oppositions are conjunctions to the opposite angle. Minor aspects like the semi-square, sesquiquadrate and quincunx may be used, but with an orb of no more than three degrees.

**Sun:** + The Sun in a harmonious aspect to the solar return horizon portends a year of great vitality, strength, and success. There is a great deal of confidence about one's work, and one tends to "shine brightly" in public. Recognition and praise are forthcoming as a result of the one's efforts, and the native tends to be highly charismatic. During this year one tends to exhibit greater leadership skills than usual, and others will tend look to him/her for direction and guidance. This is an excellent indication of good health and a strong sense of identity. Due to these factors, one is encouraged to stay close to the location where this set up is present at the time of the solar return. If the aspect to the Ascendant is not exact, one may wish to consult with a qualified professional astrologer who can advise on where this aspect would be more exact. The closer this aspect is to exact, the more powerful its correlation to life experience is likely to be.

  - Although there may be great success and recognition for one's efforts, there may also be struggles with others. One's personality may come across as too strong,  perhaps because one's need for recognition is so strong, and this can lead to conflicts with others. The native may be perceived as too arrogant, or proud, or seeking of attention and recognition. That "recognition-hunger" may be quite strong, to the extent that it may upset others around the native. One may experience an identity crisis with others who are seen as vying for credit for the same things the native is doing.

**Moon:** + This portends a year in which many positive changes can affect one with warm emotion feelings. Very intimate relationships may be cultivated, or solidified (as in marriage). One is well aware that others care greatly for him/her, and as a recipient of that love, one's own inner nature may be deeply moved. One's emotional needs can be fulfilled. In the eyes of the public, the native is held in very high regard. If one wishes to make changes in residence - either relocate or remodel the home - this year denotes success. In all matters dealing with the family or real estate, this portends favorable results. It is a year to nurture and be nurtured, to care for others and be cared for by others. It is potentially a year of a great and special love.

- This is a year that may present many special emotional challenges. One tends to be very sensitive, and perhaps easily hurt or offended, especially by those the native cares a great deal about, or by the public in general. It may be best not to take things so personally. However, if others attack one's character in a personal way, it may be hard to avoid. There could be unique and special problems involving a significant woman. Perhaps someone is too dependent upon the native, or perhaps someone the native loves is ill (i.e. mother figure). This may not be a favorable year in which to relocate the family, as adjustments to new conditions are not easy. A sense of loneliness or restlessness may be pervasive. It may be necessary to engage in intellectual pursuits in order to distract one's mind from emotional matters.

**Mercury**: + This year is favorable for communications of all kinds: writings, speeches, business transactions, negotiations, sales, and reading. The mind is highly alert and active, and very ripe for new learning - whether intellectually or in terms of learning a new skill. It is also favorable for teaching a skill to others. One is now encouraged to make deals with others, as everyone (especially the native) tends to benefit. It is also favorable for working with young people, doing any kind of detailed or analytical projects, and purchasing a new computer, computer products, or automobile. One may tend to exhibit excellent organizational skills. If one trades or invests, this tends to be favorable - especially trading.

- This year may be fraught with misunderstandings and scattered thoughts. It is necessary to stay focused on one project at a time, and not get involved in too many unrelated activities. It may also be helpful to keep records of all agreements made, for the native may change his/her mind a lot. Business deals may go sour if not communicated effectively, or if dealing with others who suffer from lack of effective communication skills. The year may also denote great restlessness, a feeling of wanting a change, but finding oneself too busy - or too uncertain - to bring it about correctly. Watch out for mistakes caused by lack of proper attention to detail. It is a year favoring learning and training, but the mind must be cleared of distractions.

**Venus:** + This is a year in which agreements and relationships of a very positive nature may unfold. In business, agreements can lead to financial success. Many new and favorable contacts and contracts may arise, and one is encouraged to pursue these. Others seem to find the native most agreeable and pleasant to be with. For the year, one exudes more than the usual grace and charm. Romantic matters also are highlighted. The native has a wonderful and appealing nature which draws others to him/her. In addition, one's personal appearance is very attractive - even the native likes the way he/she looks! Furthermore, others whom the native finds exciting and attractive come into the life, and from this, love may transpire. Things of beauty and value may also come into one's possession. Financially, one tends to do very well this year, and savings may increase, thus affording a greater sense of financial and psychological security. One is encouraged to purchase things that will make one feel "good" about him/herself, or to change the appearance in some way if wished (i.e. clothing, plastic surgery, etc.). One may function very well as a mediator between two opposing views, and receive praise from both sides. If the aspect to the Ascendant is not exact, the native may wish to consult with a qualified professional astrologer who can advise where this aspect would be more exact. The closer this aspect is to exact, the more powerful its correlation to one's life experience is likely to be.

- One may find it very hard to "look right" this year. Choosing the right combinations - for oneself or one's surroundings - may be fraught with frustration. In fact, making any decisions decisively may be a chore. There is fear of making a mistake, of choosing wrong. Because of this, one may seek advise from others, but they too may not be helpful. Be careful of advise from others, for if it doesn't work out, one may be too quick to place responsibility for the failure onto them - and that could boomerang. Others seem drawn to the native, so there is likely a high degree of charisma, but for some reason, the native simply may not feel attractive. There may also be a tendency towards procrastination, self- centeredness, and/or laziness, which may cause problems in relationships with others. It may be wise to strive for more independence and less reliance upon others this year.

**Mars**: + This is a year of great motivation to do things successfully. One tends to be highly charged, energetic, and very self-directed. One's pioneering spirit can be a great aid in starting a particular (or many) new venture(s). The native seems eager to try new things. One area that may be of great benefit is physical exercise or athletic competition - or competition of any kind this year. One tends to fare very well in such endeavors. This indicates a year of great activity, and one not given to boredom. The result of such motivation and drive is usually success in one's ventures.

- This year seems to have more than the normal amount of disputes and quarrels. Numerous battles with partners and close relations - personal and work - seem to occur. It is also a year of impetuous and perhaps immature behavior, one given towards temper tantrums. This is not favorable for relationships, and as such, close relations may be jeopardized because of the native's constant upset. In addition, one may have a tendency to act rashly and without thinking properly first. Such qualities may make one prone to mistakes or accidents. It may be wise to learn to count to ten before responding out of anger. It may also be wise to check over one's work before putting it into effect. Try not to compete with others, but rather try to find value in who they are and what they are doing. Try to reach out and help others, instead of expecting them to get out of the way. If not, they may do just that - get out of the native's way, and out of the native's life. Since this aspect tends to coincide with potentially difficult circumstances, it may be wise to consider traveling elsewhere for this solar return, a place where the Mars angular relationship would be removed altogether. If the native is open to this possibility, consult a qualified professional astrologer for assistance.

**Jupiter** +: This year may be one of great lightness and happiness. All things seem to be taken in stride, with a philosophical and positive approach. The native's demeanor appears more charitable to others, and more accepting of different points of view than one's own. For this reason, it may be easier than usual to laugh and enjoy life. Such an optimistic and flexible attitude makes one a joy for others to be around, and they may want to do more things with the native. The year therefore favors unions of all kinds - romantic, social, and professional. In many ways, one's life grows in leaps and bounds. It is a year of many successes, many opportunities, of much joy. It favors signing contracts, travel, romance, legal matters, publishing, entertainment, education, and dealings with people from foreign countries. It is one of the most fortunate positions, and one is encouraged to remain near this location at the time of this solar return. If the aspect to the Ascendant is not exact, one may wish to consult with a qualified professional astrologer who can advise on where this aspect would be more exact. The closer this aspect is to exact, the more powerful its correlation to one's life experience is likely to be.

- This is a year of many opportunities, but there may be a tendency to not follow up on these offers. Hence they may pass by. There is also a tendency to exaggerate everything and to utilize poor judgment. See things for what they really are, and not just for what one wishes of them to be. If one overestimates the goodness of others that one deals with, a loss might result. Discipline in one's behavior and personal practice are important. Over-confidence can lead to gross oversights and poor judgments, which could result in large losses. Also lack of discipline in diet can lead to weight gain. Be careful of dealings with people from different cultures. The native may be the object of a con artist. And if the native is the one attempting to con someone else out of something, he/she may get caught. One's integrity and judgment may be on the line this year.

**Saturn**: + This may be a year of great accomplishments. From these accomplishments may come a title indicating prestige and/or status (i.e. president, vice-president, etc.). One tends to command more respect as well as authority, and it is given. The native will likely handle more responsibilities now because he/she tends to be more organized and disciplined. This is a year of great maturity and professional recognition. If one has earned it (i.e. prepared well), one will get it. Long-term and positive cycles may be initiated this year. It is a time to begin realizing objectives and goals in life. One's destiny and purpose seem clearer now. Dealings with older people, or people in positions of authority, may also go well now.

- This year may be one of falling behind and constantly trying to catch up on matters of responsibility. There may be great stress and pressure, and this can lead to exhaustion, even illness. It is wise to seek balance in life, between work, exercise, and fun. Otherwise one risks "burn-out" and depression. One delay after another may prove very frustrating. There seems to be numerous obstacles to progress, and perhaps one is best advised to work on *maintaining* things, rather than trying to get ahead. It may not be a favorable year for doing things quickly. Furthermore, it is a year in which everything significant that one does is brought up for review - one is asked to account for it. This just delays things further, but perhaps it does teach you patience, and to not expect anything (otherwise one is disappointed). Since this aspect tends to coincide with potentially difficult circumstances, it may be wise to consider traveling elsewhere for this solar return, a place where this angular relationship would be removed altogether. If open to this possibility, consult a qualified professional astrologer for assistance.

**Uranus**: + This is a year of unexpected and pleasant - even marvelous - surprises. Charisma and personal magnetism, whether mental or physical, is extremely high.  As such, many new people and new ideas are attracted to the native. It is a year favoring new and exciting romances - a very "hot" year. It is also a year of many ingenious new ideas. The native can be incredibly inventive, and able to apply new thoughts to old problems, thereby coming up with wonderful new solutions. One may feel very youthful and vigorous. Romantic liaisons with people much younger than oneself could happen, or at least with people who turn the native on to new ways of looking at things, or even people whom the native turns on to new ways of looking at things. This year favors purchase of new computers or software, and a new "you", a new style.

- This is a year in which many unexpected things happen, things one did not anticipate nor plan (like a power supply failing, and losing all of one's computer data). Thus it could be filled with disruptions that make one proclaim: "Oh my God. What next?" The timing of these surprises is most likely terrible. They come when one least wishes it. One may experience separations, divorce, but at the same time attractions to new people. Unfortunately these new people may be people with whom one really has nothing in common, and hence it may not last more than 90 days. One's own timing tends to be off, and hence this is not a favorable year for speculation. One is advised to try to relate to people on their level, and not expect them to come up to the your level. Otherwise one may feel this is just a year of being very out of touch with people - one just can't relate easily, and feels like a stranger, even among friends. Since this aspect tends to coincide with potentially difficult circumstances, it may be wise to consider traveling elsewhere for the solar return, a place where this angular relationship would be removed altogether. Consult a qualified professional astrologer for assistance if interested.

**Neptune** +: This years favors romantic travels and/or experiences. It is like living a dream. Travels to tropical islands - either literally or in one's dreams - are prominent. The dream state is very active, which may be very good for imaginative efforts like advertising, writing, music, and dance. It also favors passive pleasurable and aesthetical activities like meditation, spiritual pursuits, movies, film-making, photography, reading, and plays. Acting and sailing

70

(or cruising) ventures are also favorable this year, as well as pursuits into psychic development. In the role of a counselor, one may develop and/or express great skills. There is an ability to truly help others through difficult times, and they are very grateful. If one can express compassion, he/she will likely feel a wonderful glow of love this year from others.

- This is a year of great confusion and possibly deception. One is likely very vulnerable, and a bond of trust may be broken between the native and someone the native cared for greatly. If so, tears could flow. One is easily hurt, so the native is advised to associate only with people whom are trustworthy (if one even knows who they are). In love, this is not a favorable set up. Be careful of romantic involvement with others who are already married or disloyal. Also be careful of infections and transmittable diseases. One's reputation may come up for questioning, as the native may be the object of slander and gossip, perhaps unfairly. It may be a good idea to openly talk with those who might spread such rumors, and correct them. Since this aspect tends to coincide with potentially difficult circumstances, one might consider traveling for the solar return, to a place where this angular relationship would be removed altogether. If open to this possibility, consider consulting a qualified professional astrologer for assistance.

**Pluto** +: This is a year in which one might express tremendous influence over others. One has the ability to positively affect the lives of others, to help them (and oneself) make a successful transformation at a crisis point in life. The native may be like a psychologist or detective. This could be a year of great insight and discovery. It favors research and intense study. What one discovers could be powerfully illuminating. It is favorable for getting rid of things no longer relevant to one's life, and terminating relationships that have been detrimental. It may be favorable for entering into new financial partnerships, or collecting debts owed by others. In group settings, one tends to wield much influence, and can be an agent of constructive reform reflecting the values of a larger group.

- This is a year characterized by threats. There may be a threat to one's very existence, as in a health crisis, or a dangerous situation. There may be a threat to one's position in a group, or in the community, as someone may try to undermine the native's influence. Be wary of those who might sabotage. Usually their motives are power or greed. The native must be careful of coming across coercive and intimidating, or dealing with others who are. One may deal with rejection, or feel forced into a position not sought. Since this aspect tends to coincide with potentially difficult circumstances, it may be wise to consider traveling elsewhere for the solar return, a place where this angular relationship would be removed altogether. If open to this possibility, consult a qualified professional astrologer for assistance.

# 7. CHAPTER SEVEN

## THE SIGNIFICANCE OF VOCATION AND FAMILY: ASPECTS TO THE SOLAR RETURN MERIDIAN

A planet in close aspect to the meridian - Midheaven and I.C. axis - describes influences upon one's vocation and home or family matters. It may also describe one's spiritual impetus and sense of purpose in the coming year.

An orb of six-seven degrees may be used with the major aspects (conjunction, sextile, square, or trine), and perhaps only three degrees with minor aspects (semi-square, sesquiquadrate, and quincunx). A plus (+) sign denotes the soft aspects, like sextile and trine, or conjunction involving benefics. A minus (-) sign relates to the harder aspects, like squares and conjunctions involving malefics. In the case of conjunctions or oppositions, which actually are conjunctions to the opposite angle, one may apply both the plus and minus interpretations, especially in cases involving neutral planets like the Moon, Mercury, Uranus and Neptune.

**Sun:** + This year favors recognition and success in one's profession. Along with this may come financial gains. It portends great growth and success in regards to one's work and home, which directly enhances confidence in oneself. It brings clarity to one's sense of purpose. The native tends to feel favorably identified with work, or one's "calling in life." This is a very favorable set up, and if the aspect is not exact (within 1 degree), one may wish to travel a

73

short distance (i.e. probably less than 300 miles) at the time of the solar return to bring it closer to being exact. The more exact this planetary aspect is to the meridian, the more powerful this planet's nature is likely to be in one's life this year. Consult a qualified professional astrologer for assistance in this matter if open to travel at the time of one's solar return.

- There may be conflicts both at home and work. Perhaps one causes the other. Struggles with powerful personalities may transpire over authority issues: "Who is really in charge here?" This may not be the best setup for vibrant, good health, as pressures may mount at work and transcend over to one's physical well-being.

**Moon**: + Work may have a comfortable family feeling to it, and one's family may be very supportive or helpful of the native's work this year. Both family members and work associates care a great deal about the native. One is truly blessed with love this year. Any matters dealing with real estate or relocation seem to go very smoothly. If there are changes professionally, they seem to coincide with favorable changes in income.

- This year may present serious conflicts between one's family and work duties. Demands from both may cause one to be ultra-sensitive. Relocation may not go smoothly, and one's home and/or professional life may be very unsettled. There may be a feeling of great unrest in the personal and professional life. Women at work, or at home, may be the source of great distraction or emotionalism, or they may simply be overly dependent upon the native.

**Mercury** +: This year may be one of great success in business. If the native is a business person, then he/she may see their sales and income rise nicely. One may be an excellent negotiator or deal-maker this year. The key to success is effective and timely communication. It is also an excellent year to learn or teach new skills. If one has writing ability, then a major project may be completed this year. Relationships with one's children are apt to be positive. This is a very favorable set up.

74

- Numerous deals and/or agreements seem to go awry this year. Misunderstandings seem to undermine one's business and family efforts, and it is necessary to stay clear and current with others. There may be difficulties with co-workers who seem uncooperative or petty. This may not be favorable for trading in commodities or securities.

**Venus:** + This year favors financial gains and increased income opportunities. Many new and favorable contacts may be made in one's profession, so the native is encouraged to develop relationships which have possibilities leading to professional or financial growth. There is much support for one's ideas and talents. In the context of a group, or teamwork setting, the native may be the crux of much harmony, displaying an uncanny ability to resolve conflicts so the goals of the group can be met smoothly. In fact, the native seems to have the ability to turn oppositions into allies, to make an apparent negative into a positive. Support comes from the home front as well. There is much love and sharing possible within the family structure. If one wishes to purchase or sell a home this year, great value or profit may be realized. Romantic liaisons are also possible and it may signify a year of entering into marriage or business partnerships and/or favorable agreements. This is a very favorable set up, and if the aspect is not exact (within 1 degree), one may wish to travel a short distance (i.e. probably less than 300 miles) to bring it closer to being exact. The more exact this planetary aspect is to the meridian, the more powerful this planet's nature is likely to be in one's life. Consult a qualified professional astrologer for assistance in this matter if open to traveling at this time.

- Obtaining agreements from others in work, or sale of property, may be difficult this year. It may not be easy to reach a point of compromise where all sides feel a gain. One's goals at work may be thwarted by others who are not as ambitious as the native, or perhaps are jealous of him/her. It may be the other way around too - perhaps the native is the one thwarting the goals of others. A need for compromise and a spirit of teamwork are necessary in order to complete projects successfully. One needs to be careful of distractions caused by romantic thoughts, or partners who are not carrying their fair share of responsibilities. This could correlate to a sense of falling behind in one's financial obligations.

**Mars** +: This year highlights a strong drive to accomplish goals in work, to succeed in vocational projects. The native is likely to seem very energized by work, and the more one does, the more energy he/she gets. Work may turn the native on. It is as if he/she has a passion for attaining things this year. Should one wish to become more independent at work - perhaps even begin an independent enterprise - this year is favorable for such an effort. It also suggests faring well in any area of competition. Work is not the only area in which things get done - so too are projects in the home. Perhaps there is a remodeling or building project the native has in mind. It may also be favorable for the procreation of a male child. Financially this may be an exceptional year.

- This year may be fraught with numerous battles and conflicts, both in home and at work. It may be helpful to develop more sensitivity to the effects one's actions are having upon others. Others may feel the native is making too many hasty and unwise decisions that are detrimental to the goals of the company or family. Perhaps one might ask others for their thoughts on matters before embarking upon them. Otherwise the year may find the native stepping on many toes, and upsetting those whose support may have been counted upon. The result could be loss of that support, even loss of job, as well as conflict within one's own home. This set up portends some difficult conditions during the year. One may wish to consider traveling elsewhere for the solar return in order to remove this aspect. If open to this idea, one is advised to consult with a qualified professional astrologer for assistance.

**Jupiter** +: A great deal of success and growth are possible in work and the home setting this year. Opportunities abound. There is great joy and happiness possible. Along with this comes the possibility of a large bonus or increase in income. If in business for oneself, then

76

sales probably increase greatly as a number of new accounts and contacts are developed. There is no need to go anywhere else for your solar return, as this setup is one of the most favorable possible. It is also possible that there is cause to celebrate in one's family. Perhaps it coincides with the birth of a child, grandchild, or a marriage - either the native's or someone in the native's family or social circle. Unions of many kinds are possible, and they all look favorable. This is a very propitious astrological set up, and if the aspect is not exact (within 1 degree), one may wish to travel a short distance (i.e. probably less than 300 miles) to bring it closer to being exact. The more exact this planetary aspect is to the meridian, the more powerful this planet's nature is likely to be in one's life this year. Consult a qualified professional astrologer for assistance in this matter if interested.

- Opportunities are knocking this year, but is the native listening? Be careful of overly optimistic hopes that are not fulfilled. One may be vulnerable to disappointments in others, particularly from those the native thought he/she could trust. Try not to expect so much of others this year. It may be wiser to set goals more realistically, and not so idealistically. Instead of being in a position of over-estimating the results of something, perhaps the native ought to try to under-estimate so that he/she does not fall into a position of letting others down. Agreements and contracts with others may fall short of one's expectations, so care as to whom one deals with (and the nature of those agreements) is advisable.

**Saturn:** + This is a year of gaining respect and prestige in one's work or community. One gets what is deserved, according to the amount and quality of effort that one puts into his/her duties. One may tend to be very thorough and organized, which helps in the successful completion of important projects. It also enhances the native's image as an authority or expert in his/her field. Many years of solid work (if applicable) now gives credibility and status to one's position. One's reputation in his/her field is now earned, and he/she may feel as if he/she has finally "arrived." There may also be a clarity of purpose in life, a sense of fulfillment in terms of understanding, or realizing one's "calling in life." There is a sense of self satisfaction for a job well done. Even within one's family, there seems to be a greater respect commanded or earned by the native. It is a good year to bring "honor" to one's family. One's family may now feel a sense of pride towards the native.

- This year may seem like a struggle. Tasks are difficult to complete, either because one lacks motivation to finish, or because a series of obstacles arise which cause delays. Some of these obstacles may be in the form of other people - people who may be critical in their judgment of the native's efforts, or people who are in a position to delay the results or rewards of one's efforts. Patience is necessary, and the realization that the more time it takes someone to accept one's ideas, the more time one has to either perfect his/her efforts further, or to work on other projects. There is a danger, however, that one's efforts will be rejected in total, or in part. Perhaps one should attempt to make sure that there is no danger of wasting precious time before beginning such projects, i.e. get a contract to do the job before starting it. The worst possibility is that the native is asked to do something over again, in a different way, or to modify it somehow in a manner that requires just as much work as already given. In addition to these things at work, there is also a possibility of a setback in the home or with a family member. This may not be a favorable year for moving, building a home, or taking on a new job (unless one's current position is unbearable, i.e. don't leave a "good" job, but do leave a "bad" job if possible). This set up portends some difficult conditions during the year. It may be wise to consider traveling elsewhere for the solar return in order to remove this planetary aspect to the meridian. If open to this idea, consult with a qualified professional astrologer for assistance.

**Uranus** +: This may be a year of a windfall financially or professionally. A major shift in one's work - and hence one's income - is possible. Sudden opportunities arise to move in a new direction professionally, and one is encouraged to explore this possibility. It could open up new ground, and be quite exciting. It may also lead to changes in residence. Any dealings with computers or electronics are highlighted favorably. Developments here may be favorable to one's work or career. Developments with new or old friends may also be positive, particularly as they apply to one's career or work prospects. Work seems to be a real "turn on" now, as new challenges arouse one's sense of adventure. The native may be very inspired, and thus not afraid to try new things.

- There is danger of suddenly losing one's position this year. Circumstances may arise quite suddenly - without much if any preparation possible on the native's part - and cause the native to shift his/her focus 180 degrees. These circumstances may be out of one's control - a new boss, a new owner of the company, a new landlord, etc. Or they may be a result of decisions one made that may have been off the mark. One may feel like taking risks, but this signature does not favor positive results from doing so. For instance, it tends to be unfavorable for trading of commodities or securities. It is not wise to go against company policy, or the law, or outside of one's normal "bounds." If in business for oneself, this may not bode well for taking on new products or projects without careful planning. It may be better to stay with the tried and true this year, and not try to be innovative and progressive. Important work or family contacts may leave this year, quite unexpectedly. One may be susceptible to making quick and not very-well- thought-out decisions, such as quitting work, or changing residences. Better think twice before acting on such major decisions. This set up portends some difficult conditions during the year. It may be wise to consider traveling elsewhere for this solar return in order to remove this planetary aspect to the meridian. Consider consulting with a qualified professional astrologer (who specializes in solar return relocation) for assistance.

**Neptune:** + One may find him/herself being placed upon a pedestal this year by others. Imagination in work matters, as well as domestic and family concerns, is very great. If involved in advertising or marketing, this could be quite helpful. If one designs or decorates homes or offices, this is excellent. There is a seductive "glamour" to what the native is doing that draws others in. This could be very beneficial in a sales sense, such as creating incentive programs that spurs business activity. There is a "romance" about one's work - perhaps the native really loves what he/she is doing now. It seems as if one can handle pressure quite well; in fact, one may be quite relaxed and laid back this year. Socially one will tend to do quite well too. The native is the perfect host or hostess, and everyone loves his/her parties. In both the home and work setting, one may find others come to him/her with their problems, and if the native listens carefully, they may truly be able to help others by their counsel. This can create a sense of great inner satisfaction, of knowing others were helped by one's input.

- This is a year in which one's reputation is vulnerable. One may be the subject of gossip and even slander. It is very important to conduct all of one's professional and social efforts totally above board. One must remain above reproach, for if anything is done that lets others down, they may cause great embarrassment to the native. Trust is also an important issue in all relationships and work efforts this year. One must ask of the people one is dealing with - "are they honest?". The native must also be honest in all dealings, or it will come back to haunt him/her (caught in a lie?). Take extra precautions to make sure what others are saying is understood correctly- do not assume anything that has the slightest chance of being interpreted differently by others. On the same token, one needs to be sure he/she is very clear in communications with others - do not allow them to interpret issues in any other way than what was intended. The danger this year is that a major misunderstanding could lead to great loss and/or embarrassment. This could be very disappointing to both the native and others. This set up portends some difficult conditions during the year. It may be wise to consider traveling elsewhere for this solar return in order to remove this planetary aspect to the meridian. If open to this idea, consult with a qualified professional astrologer for assistance.

**Pluto** + : This year it may be possible to work with a large and powerful group of people. The native may be given, or find him/herself in, a position of great influence. With this position, one may have the power to change things - to improve conditions - for the better. The result could be a substantial increase in profits (in business) or value/net worth (personal). Any research or investigation efforts engaged in may turn up a bonanza. This is a year of discoveries, and they prove to be very valuable to the native personally. Perhaps they result in a favorable legal or contractual or insurance settlement. Or perhaps they just give one the clout or insight needed to successfully finish projects one has been working on.

- The native may the subject of a vicious power struggle this year. One's position and status may be threatened due to the undermining tactics of another, or due to something entirely out of the native's control, i.e. illness to the native, threat of death to a family member, etc. On some level, some aspect of the native's existence may be threatened. It may be psychological or professional. One is best advised to get everything out in the open if there is a conflict brewing, so one knows who and what he/she is dealing with. There is a quality of obsession, either about the native or towards the native from another. One must learn to offer alternatives, and if the other party accepts, perhaps through mutual sacrifice a "truce" or healing may unfold. Otherwise someone may be hurt, or perhaps terminated from their position. This set up portends some difficult conditions during the year. It may be wise to consider traveling elsewhere for this solar return in order to remove this planetary aspect to the meridian. This is definitely a year in which one is advised to consult with a qualified professional astrologer for assistance, particularly an astrologer who specializes in solar return relocation.

# 8. CHAPTER EIGHT

## BEING IN THE FLOW: ASPECTS BETWEEN SAME SOLAR RETURN PLANET AND NATAL PLANET

Some years we feel totally in synch with certain aspects of our nature, and other years we feel completely out of synch. Such periods may show up in the relationship of one's solar return planets to the natal planets of the same type. Although specific aspects between the two (solar return planet and same natal planet) are most powerful, a simple analysis of gender can be quite revealing. Generally speaking, if the solar return planet is in the same sign as one's natal counter-point, the native tends to be very much in synch with that planetary principle. If the two are even in the same gender (Earth-Water are yin, or feminine, while Fire-Air are yang, or masculine), there is the sense of being compatible and in synch with this planetary principle. However, when the planets of the same type are in different genders, and especially if square or semi-square to one another, the native may feel awkward and out of synch with that principle.

We will now examine the gender relationships between the solar return and natal planets of the same type, and see the areas in which one feels in synch with natural rhythms, and which areas one may feel out of synch with those same rhythms. In those cases where the two actually make an aspect to each other, the effect is more powerful. Sextiles and trines tend to be favorable, as do most conjunctions. The squares and oppositions may be more discordant, although the opposition benefits by being in the same gender in most cases. An orb of nine degrees is allowable for most aspects between the same planets (natal to solar return). In the case of a sextile, perhaps allow only six degrees, and in the case of the more minor aspects like semi-squares, sesquiquadrates and quincunxes, allow only three.

**Moon to Moon**: When the solar return Moon aspects its own natal position, it is a year in which one's emotions and public image are highlighted.

*Same Gender*: During this year one will tend to feel fulfillment of emotional needs. One is likely to have satisfying emotional experiences, i.e. love; meeting with others who appreciate one's mannerisms, traits, or habits; social popularity, and even favorable public recognition; domestic security; happiness in moods; enjoyable experiences in eating and night-life entertainment; favorable conditions resulting from past endeavors; meeting of others with similar needs who can be helpful. There tends to be a very high degree of emotional comfort, unless the solar return Moon is afflicted elsewhere.

*Different Gender*: Obstacles, conflicts, and awkwardness in one's emotional life may be felt this year. This may result in tension and discomfort with those who are close to the native. One may tend towards moodiness, and his/her traits and mannerisms seem to upset those who are close to the native. This may be a period of social discomfort, frustrations in the domestic realm and with members of the family, associating with those who do not fulfill one's emotional needs (the native may feel hurt and/or angry at these people). This may be a year of inner struggles, blockage of basic psychological urges, and role disparity leading to erratic behavior.

**Mercury to Mercury**: When it aspects itself, especially in the conjunction, it foretells a year in which there is much mental activity and emphasis upon the native's communications and business life.

*Same Gender*: This may be a very busy year, with many decisions having to be made. Mentally, one tends to be very sharp. There is a need to communicate ideas very effectively, to get ideas across to others quite adeptly. One may be very persuasive and hard to disagree with. If inclined towards business, then it may be a year of much activity and several transactions. If inclined towards travel, especially short journeys, then there may be much travel - perhaps business-related. It is a favorable year for reading, learning, teaching, sales, and in general, getting one's ideas across to others, or being stimulated by compatible ideas from others.

*Different Gender*: One may feel more scattered in energy than usual (restless and/or nervous). The native may find little time for rest and relaxation, and is advised to make time for the latter. It also indicates a year of potential misunderstandings with others, likely resulting in annoyance and some frustration. One can help this matter greatly by adopting an open-minded, flexible, attitude towards new ideas. Basically one may feel out of synch mentally. The ideas one is accustomed to may not be readily embraced by others. Perhaps it is wise to see things from the others' viewpoint this year.

**Venus to Venus**: When Venus aspects itself, it highlights a year which emphasizes one's compatibility, relationships in general, values, possessions, and style. It may portend romance and personal attractiveness.

*Same Gender*: Compatibility with others whom the native loves and cares deeply for is highlighted this year. One may feel in a romantic mood for much of this year. Socially one may enjoy great popularity, as he/she meets people who have similar likes and dislikes. There is a sense of inner harmony and peace. There is consistency with one's psychological values, as one is in synch here. There is ample opportunity to share beautiful experiences with others. This may be a year for acquisitions which the native will value greatly, perhaps even receiving gifts and/or praise from others. Financially there may be gains and one seems on track, according to goals set for oneself. This is a year of satisfying desires, especially sensual ones. Furthermore it is a time of being treated with fairness or favoritism by others. Also one seems satisfied with their appearance and/or style. In fact, there may be favorable experiences involving one's physical appearance (increasing attractiveness i.e. hair style, new clothes, etc.).

*Different Gender*: Inharmonious situations with those whom the native loves may be experienced this year. It portends a year of disagreements, or differences in desires with those whom one wants to please. Generally speaking, this is a year of incompatibility with others, social differences, discontent with one's appearance and/or style and taste, and not being able to acquire things that give one pleasure (unless Venus is well-aspected elsewhere). There may also be a great deal of indecisiveness and hesitation in making up one's mind. Psychological conflicts regarding personal values may arise, which could cause some embarrassment. There may be problems figuring ways to please others. One is advised to be more firm and at the same time compromising with others, seeking those means that will provide the greatest balance and harmony in life, and also to avoid displays of pomp and arrogance which will be upsetting to others whom the native may be trying to please or impress. Chill out, and understand that others may not be able to be pleased all the time - nor will they always be able to please the native.

**Mars to Mars**: When Mars aspects its own natal position, it indicates a year of much impulsiveness and daring adventures; everything becomes intensified, and one may be eager (even over-eager) to start new projects.

*Same Gender*:    Conditions arise which stimulate the urge for adventure and enterprise. This is the year one has the urge to start something new in life. As such, one may experience success in new activities. One tends to feel confident and assertive. Success in competitive matters is promised, and so too is enjoyment in recreational and/or athletic endeavors. Furthermore the year highlights a passion for life, and an increase of passion in general.

85

Thus there may well be exciting and satisfying sexual experiences. There may also be a strong - even arrogant - ego nature. Basically the native is well-motivated and in synch with his/her natural physical and energy expression.

*Different Gender*: A tendency towards carelessness leading to accidents and/or disagreements (arguments) may highlight this year. There is a tendency for rashness and bluntness, perhaps causing offense to others. One is advised to be cautious of jumping into new things without thinking carefully (and consequently letting others down as the native then jumps out just as fast). One may lack foresight, thereby leaving new projects unfinished. There may be problems with self-assertiveness, obstacles in the success of new ventures - perhaps even catastrophes of sorts. One may also feel over-stimulated and/or excited. The native is advised to think before acting, to use discretion and care in all projects, especially new ones, and to practice safety in all affairs and activities where danger of accidents is even remotely possible. It may not be favorable to take an aggressive or competitive stance with others this year, as one may be out of synch with basic physical instincts. Disputes could arise that are hard to win. Even if one wins, he/she could still lose in the bigger picture.

**Jupiter to Jupiter**: When the solar return chart finds Jupiter aspecting its own natal position, a year in which one makes changes in the social life, and philosophical outlook, tend to unfold. The area of friendships are also prominent, and usually positive (unless square).

*Same gender*: Socially speaking, one is very much in synch this year. One's behavior in social situations flows naturally and easily. Thus many new unions and/or friendships may be formed. One's social life may expand nicely and the native may be invited to enter into new social circles. This year tends to highlight happy experiences with friends, and opportunities to expand one's mind, particularly the "higher" mind as in philosophy, religion, or metaphysics. In fact one feels like expanding in many areas of life,

86

depending upon the house position of Jupiter. In matters ruled by that area, there may be abundance and good fortune, wherein one feels "lucky," or at least confident.

*Different Gender*: Conflicts with friends, usually over value differences, may arise this year. Also one may experience philosophical-metaphysical-religious dilemmas, as there is a feeling of being out of synch in these areas. There may be losses through exaggeration or over-estimation and a tendency towards indulgence and excess. One may encounter criticism of their social nature by others who do not approve of the native's direction. There may be letdowns of a social nature, and in meeting others who are not what they appear to be at first. During this year one is not advised not to go to extremes in religious or philosophical matters, as this may result in great perplexities and confusion. Also one is advised to exercise discernment in the choice of new social contacts as their values may be entirely incompatible with the native's own. Do not fall for temptations that are incompatible with one's own personal morality. Don't be tempted by others into doing things that are contrary to one's own personal ethics.

**Saturn to Saturn**: It is not often that Saturn in the solar return will aspect its natal position, but in those times that it does it is very significant. These years indicate great tasks and responsibilities, leading to major accomplishments and/or much pressures.

*Same Gender*: This is perhaps a year of additional responsibilities with possible corresponding promotions. One may be in synch with responsibilities, and on track with personal and professional goals. Maturity and contentment with one's efforts and accomplishments thus far in life may be felt this year. There is a drive and opportunity to complete projects, which meets with favorable judgment by superiors or peers. There is the sense that one's life is moving in the right direction.

*Different Gender*: There may be a tendency to take on too many responsibilities and commitments during this period, or to take on tasks that are not compatible with one's basic sense of responsibilities. In other words, one may find themselves doing things they don't enjoy doing. It may be wise to start making plans for doing that which one feels is more consistent with one's goals and talents in life. The operative word is plan... not to do it now, but to start planning for a time when one can do it. Otherwise these unpleasant obligations may create feelings of limitations and frustration with one's work and/or tasks. There may be an identity crisis regarding work at this time in life, or psychological conflicts revolving around one's goals in life. There may be discontentment with work and/or employers. One is advised during this period to exercise patience, self-discipline, control and restraint, for it may seem to be a "slow" time. One is also advised to become "task-oriented" and finish up one's duties, as complaining about a situation only increases one's personal frustration. It is possible to build inner foundations now, so one may find it a favorable period to contemplate plans for the future for which this present inner building will be helpful. Giving oneself goals, however small and immediate they are, can enhance one's sense of worth, for there is a need to create a sense of accomplishment in life.

As mentioned, Uranus, Neptune and Pluto seldom aspect their natal positions, and thus an analysis of their effect is not included herein.

**Angles**: When the angles favorably aspect their respective natal positions, one seems equipped to handle situations with more ease than otherwise, whether in relationships (horizon) or work-destiny (meridian) matters.

**Ascendant-Descendant**: The relationship of the horizon in the solar return chart to its natal location describes how one interacts with one's environment and/or conditions which one has caused.

*Same gender*: This is a year of confidence and effectiveness in handling crises with others, or dealing with immediate changes in one's environment. Others tend to generally be receptive to the native. The ego is strong and there is a psychological consistency with one's attitudes. The native tends to feel in harmony with his/her environment.

*Different gender*: There may be a psychological inconsistency in one's attitudes this year, and a lack of effectiveness in handling critical situations with others. One may feel out of balance with his/her natural flow, particularly in relationships with others. The way one projects him/herself to others may feel unnatural.

**Midheaven-Nadir**: The solar return meridian in aspect to the natal meridian highlights significant attitudes about vocation, family and destiny matters.

*Same Gender*: There is a consistency between one's short-term (current year's) goals and life objectives, or long-term goals. What one is doing this year may be in harmony with one's life's calling, or work. Ideas connected with one's vocation tend to be harmonious with the life purpose (destiny). One's work and family matters may be in harmony.

*Different Gender*: Inconsistency between one's immediate or short-term goals connected with work and purpose or destiny in life may be evident this year. Are the things one is involved in consistent with his/her long-term goals, or life's calling? One's attitudes about career may be self-limiting or even defeating. There may be tension between work and family obligations. One may experience a spiritual crisis, a conflict between beliefs and duties (may have to do with something in work, or family dynamics, that violates one's personal beliefs). There may be a feeling of self-betrayal or "selling oneself out," as one may see him/herself doing something that is not really "me."

# 9. CHAPTER NINE

## SPECIFIC AREAS OF HARMONY OR STRESS: ASPECTS OF PLANETS IN A HOUSE TO THE RULER OF THAT HOUSE

A planet in a house that is in an aspect (especially major aspect) to the ruler of that same house, will indicate the ease or difficulty to be encountered in those areas of life ruled by that house, according to the nature of the aspect. Of course most of the planets in a particular house do not usually aspect the ruler of that house, but in those cases where they do the nature of the aspect will indicate whether matters pertaining to that house will go smoothly (harmonious aspect) or tend to be obstacle-forming and conflict orienting in their nature (affliction aspect). The aspects between these two planets, when they occur, take precedence over all other aspects to the planet located in the house.

This method applies to a solar return or natal planet located in a particular solar return house, in aspect to the ruling planet of that house. That ruling planet may be either the solar return or natal planet. In cases where the solar return planet falls in the same solar return house as the ruler of that house, this may be treated as a conjunction. The matters of that house are thus considered very significant for the year.

**1st house planets in aspect to rulers (natal and solar return) of 1st house:**

*Harmonious*: Generally speaking, this will be a very successful year in terms of fulfilling one's wishes for this year. One may feel ample strength and motivation in meeting all of life's challenges. One may possess a high degree of confidence and competence, and whatever tasks one commits to tend to go very well. This set up also favors generally good health, both physical and psychological. There may be a goodly amount of recognition coming to the native this year.

*Discordant*: This year may fall short of one's expectations. Recognition or attention comes, but it may not of a flattering kind. One may find he/she is the subject of criticism, probably as a result of how one expresses him/herself. It may be helpful to check out one's emotional and mental state: are you depressed? are you angry? are you too sensitive? are you too critical? If so, make an effort to overcome these negative states, otherwise others may not feel like associating closely with the native. One may also have to pay close attention to physical as well as psychological health, for this set up does not favor a healthy constitution.

## 2nd house planets in aspect to rulers:

*Harmonious*: Financial affairs tend to go very well this year. It favors appreciation of income and savings, as well as coming into possession of valuable goods.

*Discordant*: Financial affairs tend to encounter difficulties. There may be loss of money or income. There may also be a value crisis involving a significant relationship, a conflict between what one needs and what one desires. Be careful of being too gullible, or trying too hard to impress others with projections that are not consistent with one's true nature or values.

## 3rd house planets in aspect to rulers:

*Harmonious*: This year favors writing, speaking, and intellectual or mental pursuits. It favors purchase of a new automobile, or any thing that enhances communications (i.e. modem, fax machine, telephone, etc.). Relationships with neighbors and siblings may also go well this year. One is blessed with many fine and stimulating ideas. It is a year to feel inspired.

*Discordant*: Misunderstandings and difficulties in communications may mark this year. Tensions may be present in relationships with siblings or neighbors. One may experience problems with automobiles or any communications equipment (i.e. computers, telephones, fax machines, etc.).

## 4th house planets in aspect to rulers:

*Harmonious*: Harmonious conditions are experienced in the home and family. This favors family gatherings, and any changes involving one's household. Perhaps a change of residence, or birth of a child is forthcoming. It is also favorable for getting in tune with one spiritual self. It portends a deepening of consciousness, getting in touch with one's essence and inner, basic needs.

*Discordant*: This year may be fraught with domestic troubles. There tends to be a very unsettling feeling to one's residence and/or family. Close relationships may sour. In addition, there may be an inner, or spiritual crisis. It may be wise to spend time in meditation and reflection during this year. It is generally not a favorable time to relocate, or it may indicate structural problems with the residence currently occupied.

## 5th house planets in aspect to rulers:

*Harmonious*: This year indicates excellent relations with one's children. It is generally a very happy and creative year, filled with many pleasurable experiences in one's social life. It favors romance and play. Entertaining, and going out to see entertainment, is favorable this year. All in all, it is a marvelous time to enjoy oneself. If the native speculates, he/she may experience much success. Socially, one may be very popular.

*Discordant*: The year inclines towards difficulties with one's children, or in the field of romance. Romance may go sour. One may tire of another (or at least one party tires of the other). Or, one may be attracted to incompatible types. The native find him/herself with others who demand things that are incompatible with one's own basic needs. One is encouraged to avoid chasing others, or acting like a "groupie." One should like him/herself for who he/she is, and not try to become like others in hopes of being better liked. Otherwise one may not fare too well socially.

## 6th house planets in aspect to rulers:

*Harmonious*: One will tend to enjoy work this year. Not necessarily the profession or the people one works for, but the tasks that one is assigned or asked to do are enjoyable and fulfilling. This is a good year to take pride in what one does, for one tends to do very good work. If one is a craftsman, then one's skill appreciates greatly this year, and others comment on this. One also tends to get along well with their fellow co-workers. There is a spirit of cooperation and teamwork that emanates from the native. This placement also bodes well for one's health and diet, for it represents a more sensitive awareness of one's bodily needs.

*Discordant*: One may be easily annoyed or irritated with either their own performance, or the performance of others this year. The native may be hard to please, and likewise, he/she may find it hard to please others. These tensions may result in physical exhaustion, stress, or ill health. The cause of these problems may be in boredom. Perhaps one's life has fallen into a rut, an unexciting routine of the same daily grind. If so, one may need to challenge him/herself, and simply force a "break" in self-imposed and self-limiting structures. Get out and play more. Find something in life that excites. Learn a craft. Otherwise these self-induced frustrations may cause others who care about the native to plan activities without him/her, thus leaving the native out altogether. The native may thus may feel betrayed and/or lonely.

93

## 7th house planets in aspect to rulers:

*Harmonious*: This year favors excellent partnerships and marriage. The native and his/her partner(s) may be getting along splendidly. If one has no partners, then this year may find one being formed. It favors entering into agreements, and forming alliances with people who represent the native well. It may be a good year to find an excellent attorney, if there is a need for one. If married, one's partner tends to do very well, and this strengthens one's marriage. It is also a year favoring popularity and social advancement.

*Discordant*: There may be difficulties in partnerships this year. One's marriage may encounter new challenges. These challenges may threaten any partnership - business or marriage. Contracts may not go through, or may not honored, so be cautious of any agreements made or contemplated. One's partner(s) may have personal problems this year which affect the native's relationship to them. This is the year that one reaps the results of unhealthy projects sown previously. This is karma that somewhere along the line the native has created, and now his/her own evolution depends upon overcoming prior patterns to resolve it.

## 8th house planets in aspect to rulers:

*Harmonious*: This year presents an opportunity to get out of unhealthy and/or unproductive relationships that have been plaguing the native. Matters of great difficulty may now be brought to a culmination, and successfully terminated - at least terminated for one's own good. Matters to do with taxes, insurance and estate settlements may work in the native's favor, and from these he/she may receive sizable monies. If engaged in research efforts, there is much of value waiting to be discovered. It is a year of insight. It is also a year that may highlight exciting and satisfying sexual activity. One may be given, or have earned, a position of influence and power as well.

94

*Discordant*: This may be a year of financial stress. Monies owed to the native cannot be collected. Or, one may have loans outstanding which are hard to repay. In addition, there may be conflicts between what one really wants to do, and the demands and obligations one feels others make upon him/her. Be careful of a tendency to blame others for one's present status. One does have a choice, and one is making it. Affairs may end this year, perhaps against one's will. One may be the subject of a power play, so "know thy enemies" (if there are any), and get them to put all the cards on the table. What one does not want is to find someone undermining the native's efforts without the native's knowledge. For that matter, someone may be investigating the native or his/her background without one's permission. There may be problems with taxes, insurance claims, and estate matters. In addition, sexual activities may be dissatisfying, or lead to problems. Be cautious and discerning now.

## 9th house planets in aspect to rulers:

*Harmonious*: The year generally tends towards happiness and lightness of being. If involved in publishing, litigation, or educational efforts, they tend to come out very favorable. Relations with people from different ethnic backgrounds also fare well. It is an excellent year for long distance or foreign travels. One's philosophical interests are stimulated as one comes into contact with many new ideas. This is a good year to expand one's social circle with people of different backgrounds and philosophies. All matters involving education or legal areas tend to be successful.

*Discordant*: This year one may experience a philosophical crisis, or perhaps a religious or spiritual conflict. There may be difficulties in education as well. School, or training may be hard, and if so, one needs to give more time to it. Legal matters do not proceed smoothly; in fact, they may come out against the native. There may also be delays or rejection in publishing ventures. It is wise to avoid litigation matters this year if at all possible, and perhaps be more conscientious of educational responsibilities and goals.

## 10th house planets in aspect to rulers:

*Harmonious*: Great successes in one's vocation are highlighted this year. It signifies realization of goals and completion of projects. There may also be an increase in status, perhaps a title of some sort is given to the native. One is earning a fine reputation in the profession or community, and others are showing respect and admiration for the native's achievements.

*Discordant*: Conflicts with regard to one's profession may be encountered. The native may question whether or not this is really what one wants to do. The trouble is, it may not be a favorable time for changing. Conflicts with superiors may arise, and if not careful, this could result in job loss. It may be time to closely examine what one is doing, and what one's real goals in life are. If one does not support the other, it may be time to start exploring other options that will bring one back into harmony with his/her own sense of destiny and purpose in life. To continue on the present path may result in frustration, and the feeling that "time is passing me by."

## 11th house planets, in aspect to rulers:

*Harmonious*: This year may highlight the results of successful efforts in the past (or present). It is not the effort itself, but the results or rewards that come from it (i.e. income, new position with greater authority). It also favors group activities. These group activities are not only enjoyable, but they add a richness to one's life. New friendships may be formed now, and old ones may be solidified with new and enriching experiences.

*Discordant*: This year one may encounter power plays in groups. These power plays cause one to examine his/her motives and reasons for being in the group. Is the native there for the personal glory it may bring, or because he/she believes in its objectives and goals? Conflicts with friends may also unfold, and one is encouraged to be sensitive to their needs (or they to the native's). Otherwise there may be a loss of a close friend.

## 12th house planets in aspect to rulers:

*Harmonious*: This year favors quiet and freedom from disruption. It is excellent for research, or for a retreat, or for quiet time. Plan to go away for awhile where no one is known. It favors helping others through expressing sympathy. It is a year of many dreams and heightened intuition. If artistically inclined, it could be quite favorable for any efforts in this area.

*Discordant*: In retrospect, one may look back and wonder if this year was somehow lost. It may have been a year of much promise, but nothing happened. This is moreso perhaps if planets in the twelfth house afflict the ruler of the Ascendant. But in both cases, the signatures suggest a possibility of unfavorable dealings with institutions like jails, prisons, hospitals, and other places of confinement. One's worst enemy may be the fears inside of one's own mind. One's dreams may be very disturbing, and it wise not to engage in over-active fantasies and unrealistic, delusional, thinking.

**Example**: Let's use the author's son to illustrate this technique. Sean was born January 27, 1986, Southfield, Michigan, 10:26 PM. His 12th solar return was celebrated at home, in Farmington Hills, MI., January 27, 1998. The solar return chart is shown in Figure 7, with Solar Return angles, and natal planets in the outer wheel.

Note in this chart that he has natal Uranus posited in the solar return fourth house. The 4th house is Sagittarius, which means Jupiter is the ruler. Both his natal and solar return Jupiter are in late Aquarius (a Jupiter return as well in the 12th year). These two Jupiters - which rule the 4th house of this chart- form a sextile to his natal Uranus which is in the fourth house. Therefore he will tend to experience harmonious events in the home and family for the year, which are fourth house matters. His relationships with at least one of his parents is apt to go very well (hopefully with both his parents). His fifth house is not as well aspected. Here Saturn rules (Capricorn on the cusp). The solar return Saturn is posited in the 8th house, and in square aspect to the Venus and Mercury of his

97

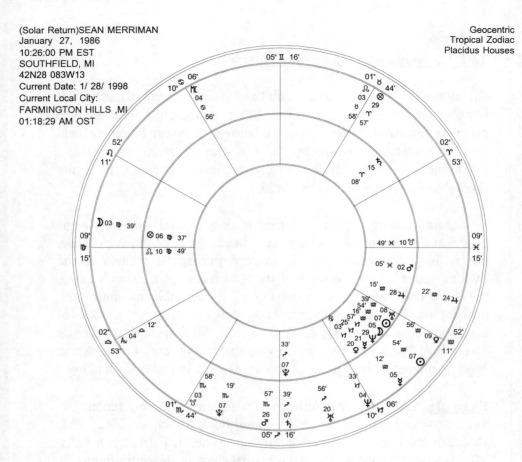

(Solar Return)SEAN MERRIMAN
January 27, 1986
10:26:00 PM EST
SOUTHFIELD, MI
42N28 083W13
Current Date: 1/ 28/ 1998
Current Local City:
FARMINGTON HILLS ,MI
01:18:29 AM OST

Geocentric
Tropical Zodiac
Placidus Houses

**Figure 7: 12th Solar return for author's son.**

solar return fifth house. However his natal Saturn is in early
Sagittarius, in sextile to the solar return Sun, Moon, and Uranus
which are also posited in the fifth house. He is apt to experience a
multitude of events - both harmonious and challenging - in matters
to do with the opposite sex this year. In fact it is the year of his first
girlfriend. The sixth house finds both natal and Solar Return Jupiter,
and both in sextile to natal Uranus which rules this house.
Therefore his work is likely to improve, and possibly his knowledge
of health, diet, and nutrition will increase as well.

# 10. CHAPTER TEN

# TIME BANDS OF SPECIAL IMPORTANCE WITHIN THE YEAR: THE PROGRESSED SOLAR RETURN MOON

The art of predicting events - or changes - and the timing of those events by means of the solar return chart is a three-fold process. The first of these, the progressed solar return Moon, will be discussed initially, whereas transits and the "one degree per day angular progression" methods will follow.

### THE PROGRESSED SOLAR RETURN MOON

The assumption in secondary progressions is that one day, or one complete rotation of the Earth on its own axes, is the equivalent of one year of life. This premise applies also to the solar return chart. By determining the daily motion of each planet for the 24-hour period following the moment of the solar return, and then dividing this motion by twelve months, one may ascertain the monthly motion - and hence the monthly position - of each planet to the nearest minute of arc. In fact if one wishes, even the daily position of the progressed solar return planets may be ascertained. However, as planets other than the Moon progress so slowly in one day (or one solar return or one progressed year), and thus so few exact aspects will be formed from them in a given year (except in those cases, perhaps, where two planets are located in very close aspect, like within one degree), there is very little use in finding the monthly positions of any of the progressed planets other than the solar return Moon.

The progressed solar return Moon (which is the equivalent of the Moon's daily motion in the 24-hour period during the moment of solar return) may move at a rate of slightly less than 12 degrees to slightly more than 15 degrees in a given year. At this rate, several additional aspects may form to solar return and natal planets and their solstice points. Thus it is necessary to pinpoint the progressed Moon's monthly position in order to determine when the influence is in effect.

With the advent of computers and software programs (like Seek-It Publication's Solar Return program by the author), it is no longer necessary to calculate these positions - and aspects - by hand. The Solar Return program calculates the exact date in which the progressed solar return Moon makes exact aspects to other solar return and natal planets, and their solstice points. In the case of solstice points, calculations only to the major aspects appear to be the most reliable.

When determining the dates in which the progressed solar return Moon makes exact aspects in the course of a given year, it is necessary to note two things. First, allow an orb of six weeks before and after each date, as these progressed lunar aspects have a time band in which they may be effective. In most cases only three weeks either side of the exact aspect will suffice, but in some cases this may be extended out to as much as six weeks, especially in those cases where a supportive transiting aspect of a similar type comes into play. Second, the calculation period to be covered should include three months before the actual solar return date, through 15 months following it. In other words, it should cover an 18-month time band.

The reason for this is that one's life doesn't just suddenly change on the solar return birthday. There is a transition phase in which the conditions and issues of the previous year (as shown in the previous year's solar return) begin to give way to the new conditions and issues denoted by the current year's solar return. According to the principles developed by this author in the original *Solar Return*

100

*Book of Prediction*, this transition phase begins three months prior to one's birthday, and continues for three months following the next year's birthday. That is, three months prior to a solar return (when transiting Sun applies to a square to the natal Sun), one begins to witness the issues and conditions arising that will be relevant during the next birth year. Furthermore, the issues one is working through in any solar return year, will continue to be of importance for about three months following the *next* solar return (when the transiting Sun forms the waxing square to the natal Sun). One doesn't just leave those issues at once at the time of the birthday. During the three months before and after the birthday, there is this transition period where the conditions of the past begin to be resolved (or require less and less attention), and the new conditions and issues - shown in the new chart -  begin to command increasingly more attention.

For those who do not have a solar return software program to calculate these aspects, the rules for determining the position of the progressed solar return Moon at any time are as follows (using a midnight, GMT, ephemeris):

I. Subtract the midnight longitude of the Moon on the day of the solar return (GMT) from the midnight longitude of the Moon on the day after the solar return.

II. Convert this result to total minutes (multiply the  degrees by 60 minutes and add to remainder of minutes).

III. Divide this total by 12 (months) to determine the monthly motion of the progressed Moon. If result is over 60 minutes, convert back into degrees and minutes.

IV. Starting with the Moon's longitude on the solar return birthday, add the progressed Moon's monthly motion, cumulatively, for twelve months. Each result will pertain to the same day, of the following month, for each of the twelve months following the solar return date.

V. Record these monthly positions of the solar return progressed Moon, and determine which months the progressed Moon will make exact aspects to other solar return or natal planets and their angles, and even their solstice points. These months, then, will be highlighted during the year according to the type of aspect formed, the planet or angle being aspected, and the houses involved.

The formula for finding the solstice point of any planet or angle is a two-fold process. First, convert the given sign of the zodiac to the corresponding solstice sign as follows:

Aries = Virgo      Taurus = Leo        Gemini = Cancer

Libra = Pisces    Scorpio = Aquarius    Sagittarius = Capricorn

Next, subtract the given planet's, or angle's, degree and minute from 30 degrees, or 29 degrees and 60 minutes.

As an example, assume one has a solar return Venus at 10 degrees, 19 minutes of Virgo, and solar return Moon at 17 degrees and 40 minutes of Cancer. Where would the solstice point of Venus be, and when would it be in aspect to the progressed solar return Moon? The first step would be to convert the solar return sign of Venus to its solstice sign. Virgo = Aries, so we know its solstice point would be in Virgo. Second, subtract the planet's degree and minute from 30 degrees (or 29 degrees, 60 minutes). Since its degree and minute was 10 degrees and 19 minutes, it's solstice degree and minute would be 19 degrees and 41 minutes. Thus the solstice point of 10 Virgo 19 would be 19 Aries 41. In two months (at the rate of one degree per month), the progressed solar return Moon would square this Venus solstice point, and in all likelihood, an event of this nature would transpire within six weeks of being exact (perhaps a disappointment in a love matter, or a problem with a woman).

This then gives the solstice points of the natal and solar return planets and angles. When the solar return Moon is progressed, exact dates of aspects to both the natal and solar return planets and their solstice points should be noted. Minor aspects like the semi-square, sesquiquadrate, and quincunx can be noted with the "normal" planets, along with the major aspects. They may have a minor influence. However, when determining aspects to the solstice point planets and angles, one is advised to use only the major aspects, such as conjunction, square, trine, and opposition.

When calculating the lunar aspects that are in effect up to three months prior to one's solar return, it is necessary to actually utilize a technique called "converse progressions". Here, one simply takes the monthly movement of the progressed solar return Moon (as already calculated), and subtracts this amount each month from the solar return Moon's position - up to three months prior to the birthdate. One can then list these progressed dates in chronological order, beginning with three months before the solar return date - i.e. converse progression, indicating where the Moon was up to six hours before the solar return, and which aspects were in effect - and continuing for the following 30 hours after the solar return (i.e. equivalent of 15 months after the birthdate). Next to the date of the aspect, one might list the planet - or planet's solstice point - that the progressed solar return Moon is aspecting.

The following represent the meanings - the issues, types of conditions, and types of people - that the native will tend to experience during the periods in which the progressed solar return Moon makes an aspect to the listed solar return or natal planet or angle, or their solstice points. The plus (+) sign refers to the soft aspects, like the sextile and trine, or a conjunction involving a benefic, but not involving malefics. The minus (-) sign represents the more difficult aspects, such as the square and opposition, minor aspects like the semi-square, sesquiquadrate, and quincunx. It may also pertain to conjunctions involving malefics, especially to one another. From the date in which the aspect is exact, use an orb of six weeks either side (usually three weeks either side will suffice). During that time band, transits to either the solar return or natal planets will help narrow the timing down even further.

## Sun (natal or solstice point):

\+ During this period one will tend to feel a sense of harmony and success in all efforts. Changes for the better are likely in regards to career, family, and close relationships. One's health may improve, and greater energy and vitality may be noticed. The native tends to shine in situations which require leadership, and others may look to the native for direction. Overall it is a time of confidence, potential recognition, and creative self-expression. It is a time when one is likely to feel as if he/she is growing, or has grown, and many activities are coming to fruition in a successful manner.

\- One may now feel very restless and unsettled. It is important to keep the mind focused and challenged. Matters to do with one's work or home life may require additional attention as several changes may be unfolding. One may not have anticipated these changes, and as such may be rather moody - or emotional - regarding them. Try to be flexible and open-minded. If one worries too much, he/she may become exhausted. This could lead to a decline in physical energy, even illness. If close relationships are going through a troublesome period, try to be more caring or nurturing. Understand that the native him/herself too may require the same of someone else, but it is best not to be too dependent. In fact, dependencies may be the source of the problem: either the native - or a significant other - may be too dependent upon the other, perhaps causing a sense of "smothering." Changes are probably happening, and they may be out of the native's control, and the best approach may be to develop a sense of "acceptance", and quickly adapt to these "new" conditions. If one doesn't accept these changes over which there is no control, the native may find him/herself frustrated and unhappy, and that sort of whining may cause others to withhold the support the native craves.

## Moon (only Solar Return to Natal position):

\+ Within six weeks of this date, one may feel a great and special love for - and from - someone special. This arouses the closeness and intimacy drive. This is a fine time to do very special things with people whom one cares a great deal about. These experiences may be deeply cherished, and remembered fondly. It is an excellent period for family activities and any domestic changes one wishes to make (i.e. renovation, moving, fertility, pets, etc.). A bond is likely strengthened between the native and someone special. It is a time when one can depend upon others, and they can depend upon the native.

- Within six weeks of this date, one may feel very restless and emotional. Feelings tend to be easily hurt, and one may be given to bouts of whining, complaining, anger, or even crying. Close relationships may be a source of difficulties: perhaps one is too dependent upon them, or feeling suffocated because they are too dependent upon the native. Family matters may also be troubling. During this period one is encouraged to examine his/her life and determine areas where one can be truly thankful and grateful. Instead of seeing oneself as a victim, perhaps the native could see him/herself as someone who is fortunate for the things and relationships in life that are working out well. An attitude of appreciation and thankfulness is very possible, and will endear the native to others, rather than the alternative, which is to push others away through a quality of over-clinging. It would also be helpful to have a specific and challenging project to focus upon. Otherwise one may be troubled by boredom, restlessness, or too many conflicting and undirected thoughts.

**Mercury:**

+ (include conjunction here): Within six weeks, changes for the better are possible in regards to one's work or service. A period of great mental acuity may commence in which one's mind is apt to be sharp and quick. The native may have the opportunity to make very good deals, as this is a positive business decision aspect. Life - and work - may be quite busy, but the native probably enjoys this activity. It is an excellent time to write, speak, teach, learn, and in general it favors all types of communications and travel. Should one

105

have need for a new automobile, computer, software program, or any devise that enhances communications, this is an excellent time for purchase. News may come out that is positive. It also favors any activities with young people.

- Within six weeks of this date one may encounter some sort of misunderstanding with another. Difficulty may be experienced in getting ideas - or intent - understood by others. Others too may feel the native does not understand their position. Adjustments may be necessary, and one may have to act quickly (but not rashly) in order to get everything back on track. During this period, the native is encouraged to make certain of facts, and not project blame onto others without checking things out first. Business decisions, deals, or activities may go sour, due to misunderstandings or misinformation. It is possible to salvage something, though, if one adjusts quickly to the new reality. Carefulness in signing of papers or making any agreements only after thorough analysis and total understanding is advised. Also one may need to be careful of others who may try to attribute thoughts to the native that he/she did not express.

**Venus**:

+ Within six weeks of this date, one may experience much popularity, romance, and acceptance. One's magnetism may be very strong during this period, and others may just want to do things with the native. It favors contracts, agreements, and social activities. Others are very supportive and helpful in one's efforts and with regard to one's needs. Perhaps the native makes a large item consumer goods purchase, or is given something of great value. It is also favorable for any changes in appearance and style. Matters of love and romance are highlighted favorably during this time. So too are positive financial developments. Perhaps there is a pay raise, or increase in sales, or just the realization that one's savings and net worth are increasing. It can coincide with a sense of greater financial and psychological security, as well as amorous feelings of attraction to and from another.

106

- Within six weeks of this date one may feel uninspired, lazy, and lethargic. One may feel amorous, like they would like love in their life, but either relationships are not terribly exciting, or else the native may not be acting with much enthusiasm. Perhaps "the right" person is not around, or if she/he is, then perhaps the relationship is having difficulties. This may be a period of great indecision and wavering. Taking too long to make up one's mind could be costly. Opportunities may disappear or be withdrawn. Furthermore one may not feel very attractive. The native may be hard to please. This is not a favorable time to make large purchases, or to radically alter one's appearance or style, although some amount of shopping may be helpful to the spirit temporarily. It may be in one's best interest to be more independent, and less reliant upon others now. It may also be useful to clearly think out what one wants in regards to others, and to clearly express these thoughts to them - especially in business matters, but also in personal relationships. One can meet people now, but it may be wise to tread carefully before making any commitments.

**Mars:**

+ Within six weeks of this date one may feel very energetic and highly motivated. Many of one's activities seem to be going great, and much of one's success is due to the native's own enthusiasm and hard efforts. During this period one may either start new ventures, or find him/herself thoroughly immersed - and enjoying - things that have recently been started. There is a sense of "newness" and adventurousness all about. There is also a healthy sense of competition, and one may fare well in activities with or against others. One may have a "passion" for life, and in fact physical passions may be highly aroused. In addition, one may exhibit very fine leadership skills, combined with a healthy, pioneering spirit. This is an excellent time to plan things that one wants to go well.

- Within six weeks of this date one may feel very testy, argumentative, and combatant. As result, one may have more than the usual number of quarrels and disputes with others. Accidents

107

could happen, so it is best to be cautious and even defensive, to take one's time with getting to places. Rushing through things could result in errors and a need to do them over again, not to mention how one may tend to react to such events (i.e. could be quite upsetting). This is a period in which meditation may be very beneficial. It is certainly a time in which one should carefully review everything before putting it into motion. This is not the most favorable time for starting new projects. However one may have ample energy and passion - just try to direct it positively.

**Jupiter:**

+ Within six weeks of this date one may experience a great deal of success and/or happiness in all affairs. This is a time of celebration and joy. Perhaps there are many occasions to socialize or party with friends or family. There may be weddings, announcements of births, or other special occasions with which to celebrate. Or, it may be just a very active and pleasurable social period. One's attitude of friendliness and positive thinking helps in all dealings with others. There may be gains through work, contracts, and agreements. Unions with people and long journeys are positive now as well. This is a time of expansion and success, bringing about great happiness in general. If the native is in school, or learning or teaching something of value, or traveling, the experience tends to be very positive. This is a time of confidence and "good feeling."

- Within six weeks of this date, one may experience a tendency to exaggerate or over-reach in activities. One may find he/she has taken on too many things. One's judgment - both in others and in regards to how much can be handled - may not be accurate. One is advised to try not to over-estimate him/herself, others, or what one can or cannot do. It is possible that one could feel quite confident - in fact, over-confident. It favors socializing and meeting people, having a good time. However one needs to be careful of speaking without thinking, for he/she could unintentionally insult others and/or bring embarrassment to the self. It may be a time of indulgence and excess, of giving into temptation and forsaking

108

discipline. It is therefore not the best time to make agreements or sign contracts - one may be giving away too much and this could result in loss.

**Saturn**:

+: Within six weeks of this date, one may tend to feel very organized and in control. There may be the realization that long-term efforts are paying off. Perhaps credit is coming in the form of recognition, greater income, status, or new responsibilities and authority. One has earned the respect of others for his/her accomplishments, dedication, and commitment, and may now be seen as an expert, or authority in their field. This is a time period in which the native may feel as if a certain plateau, or goal, or level in life has been achieved, and it is satisfying.

- Within six weeks of this date, one may have feelings of frustration, as if stuck or blocked in something that is important. Things may not be moving as quickly or smoothly as hoped. There is a tendency for delays, and thoughts of totally giving up on these projects may be entertained. Perhaps one is too critical of their own efforts. Worse yet, perhaps others are too critical, and that could elicit feelings of hurt. Be careful of feelings of inadequacy, or incompetency. The native may now need a strong support group - or person - to remind him/her of his/her positive and good personal qualities. It may be very beneficial for the native to reach out and try to help someone now. This can help resurrect feelings of value and self-worth. It is not advantageous to spend time with others who are critical and hard to please; it will only put one into a further spin. Likewise, it is not wise for the native to behave that way: being too critical and hard to please may cause others to avoid contact with him/her. Feelings of loneliness, or alone-ness, may be prevalent, and to counter-act them, one might consider forcing him/herself to get out and away from personal worries. The native may not feel like socializing, so perhaps going to movies or reading a good book that has morally strong characters could be positive. One may be going through a moral dilemma, but the results could be quite positive, yielding a stronger and more clear set of principles for one's own conduct and self-respect. This is a reflective time, but one in which the native is advised to try to avoid spending too much time on worry, for it probably doesn't solve anything, and may lead to greater depression.

**Uranus**:

+ : Within six weeks of this date, one is apt to feel great excitement in life. It is as if the native has suddenly been turned on. There are great new ideas, in fact perhaps some kind of breakthrough - either in work life, social life, or mental outlook. This is an inventive period. New possibilities come to mind. As the native taps into this new awareness, he/she becomes very magnetic to others. They are now attracted to the native, turned on by his/her energy. This period favors computers, technology, travel, new automobiles, new adventures, and new friends or romance. Extraordinary things can happen, and this creates much youthful vigor and excitement.

- : Within six weeks of this date, it may seem as if a series of disruptions and distractions are suddenly occurring. Everything seems to fall apart or come unraveled at once. People are strange. They act erratically and perhaps without reason or sensibility. Even the native is given to erratic behavior and emotionalism. One day the native is up and the next day down. This period may coincide with separations and disagreements. It may be difficult to see eye to eye with others. One is just on a different track, and one's timing may be off. Still, there are plenty of exiting new ideas. It is a time of progressive thinking. It's just that nobody can understand or appreciate what the native is conceiving. It is difficult getting ideas across effectively, and so the native may feel awkward and out of place. He/she may meet people who are exciting, at least physically attractive, but may also discover there is nothing really in common with them. It may be best to use this period to write ideas down and come back to them later (they are ahead of their times, perhaps). This may not be a favorable period in which to make new purchases in computers or electronics, for all such matters (and electrical ones

110

too) may go awry. What one is attracted to, and what one thinks they want, may not be accurate now.

**Neptune**:

+ : Within six weeks of this date, one may feel very romantic. The imaginative part of the mind is stimulated, and the native may "see" or visualize things very vividly. If one is inclined towards the arts or music or writing, this may be a wonderfully creative period. If one has spiritual leanings, this may be a time of a marvelous outpouring of compassion, one that cleanses the soul, so to speak. There is an "opening" on an inner level, a "heart" experience. This period favors vacations and travel, especially to romantic areas, or tropical climates, or areas near water and nature. This is an excellent time to go out and entertain, or be entertained. Experiences around glamorous individuals or activities may be quite enthralling. As a counselor, one may experience an encounter with someone who is truly grateful for the native's help. There is a joy at knowing one has really helped someone. The native's behavior may be saintly or virtuous, or he/she may meet someone who behaves that way to them. This is a time to be gentle with others - there is something precious in one's life. Recognize what that is.

- : Within six weeks of this date, the native may feel as if in a fog, out-of-touch, and distracted by thoughts other than what is happening right in front of oneself. It is necessary to harness all of one's energy to keep focused. The native may be vulnerable to deception and even betrayal, but can probably prevent this by just noticing the signs as they arise. If the native does notice, then talking to these individuals before they do harm may prevent it. There is a need to clear up any misunderstandings between the native and others. One is likely to be very imaginative now, and this could be positive in an artistic sense. However one may also be given to fantasies and delusional thinking, so before fully believing in something, it may be wise to make sure there is a basis in reality for that belief. The native may be well-advised to avoid gossip or talking negatively about others, as it may come back to haunt him/her. One's "secrets" are not likely to be held in confidence, so one must be careful of what is said and to whom it is said. The native's reputation may be on the line, and he/she may be the subject of false accusations or deceptions. One needs to try and see things as they are, and check out intuition with reality during this time.

**Pluto**:

+ Within six weeks of this time one is likely to experience some deep insight or a sense of power, or both. This may be a time of revelation, of discovering something, of finding out something of value. In group settings, one may have considerable influence over others, and with this influence, may be an agent of some kind of change, reform, or improvement. This period may be most marked by successful efforts to bring something to a close. It favors terminations, eliminations, and transformations - or changes for the better. It is also a period in which one may experience satisfying sexual activity. Financially it bodes well too, particularly to those in sales, and it favors opening new accounts. It also favors collecting debts or getting a mortgage or loan approval.

- Within six weeks of this date, one may encounter an intense battle with someone, or a battle with someone who is very intense. There may be a threat of some kind - perhaps to the native's position, maybe even to the life of someone close by to the native. One's feelings are likely to be very intense, and the behavior may be somewhat obsessive. It may be helpful for one to try to see alternatives to decisions that affect others adversely. Rejection may play a key role now. One could be the recipient or cause of that. On a positive note, it favors research so long as that which is sought is not for the intent of using against someone else. There may be problems in the areas of taxes or insurance or debt collection. If the native owes monies, it is better try to pay up if possible. If others owe the native, do not expect payment now. It is not favorable to loan or borrow money now. In terms of personal relationships, it may be wise to be more sensitive and gentle. Any forcefulness on the part of the native will not be met with approval. In addition, one is encouraged to avoid coercive individuals, and to not share confidences with those not trusted.

**Ascendant/Descendant** (both natal and solar return...conjunction and opposition are positive):

+ : Within three months of this date one may notice positive changes within the home and close relationships. One tends to feel an increase in affection for others, and from them as well. Improvements in the family and domestic setting are possible. The native's power of attraction to others is quite strong. This favors romance, dealings with women, and an increase in a close, intimate bond with someone special.

- : Within three months of this date one may feel rather scattered and more emotional than usual. This tends to be a restless period, and the native is encouraged to find something of value to engage his/her mental energies. One may be over-sensitive to those closest to him/her, and perhaps should talk to them about these feelings. The may be a great need to be loved now, but also a knack of driving others away by being too needy or dependent.

**Midheaven/Nadir** (both natal and solar return, conjunction and opposition are both positive and negative):

+ : Within three months of this date, one may experience changes for the better in work and/or home. Yet this may be accompanied by a great deal of worry and restlessness if the aspect is a conjunction or opposition. There is much support for changes here. Whether the native actually changes career, or just works on different projects within the same role, the change appear beneficial. There is a feeling of "family" with those whom one works. At home there is a special bond between the native and his/her spouse, children, parents, or whomever the native might live with. One's nurturing qualities are appreciated by others. This period favors changes in residence.

113

- : Within three months of this date, one may feel very restless with work or family roles. The native tends to be moody both at work and at home. There may be something unfulfilling about what one is doing. It may be a slow time, or one filled with unchallenging tasks. Perhaps it is best to take a relaxed and patient attitude about these things. They are likely to pass, and one's tendency to complain or whine isn't likely to help matters out. In fact, it may turn things worse. This may not be a favorable time to relocate or move. Changes within the family or work are not advised just yet. One's emotional needs tend to be great, and perhaps one should discuss these with the mate, if married or in love. It may be useful to be more independent right now, and not to depend upon others who don't seem to deliver what is needed or sought.

# 11. CHAPTER ELEVEN

## SHORT-TERM CYCLES: TRANSITING SUN THROUGH THE SOLAR RETURN HOUSES

Since the solar return is based upon the movement of the Sun (actually the earth in relationship to the Sun), it is logical to assume that the transiting position of the Sun in relationship to the solar return chart would be important. And it is.

The transiting Sun in aspect to natal planets highlights a short period of time of significance during the year. So too does the transiting Sun in aspect to the planets in the solar return chart. They are similar in their influence, and in the duration of time in which they are in close aspect to one another, which is only 1-3 days.

An area that will be considerably different, however, is the importance of the transiting Sun through the solar return houses. Although the entire period during which the transiting Sun through a house emphasizes conditions dealing with that house, it is primarily the three-day period surrounding that house ingress that is most important. Three days before through three days after the time the transiting Sun conjuncts a solar return house cusp brings to the forefront conditions involving that house's domain.

The following is a delineation of those periods in which the transiting Sun travels through the houses of the solar return chart during the year in effect. It describes what to expect during these time bands, which may start up to three days before actually entering that particular house.

**The Transiting Sun In The First House**: During this period the native will tend to be more in the limelight. He/she will tend to be more confident, radiant, energetic, and charismatic. One's role as a leader in his/her surroundings will tend to be more acknowledged by others, and accepted by the native him/herself. One's motivation to do things better and more successfully is stronger; one is likely to be more assertive and creative, as well as more directed in all efforts. This time band favors good health and positive recognition.

**The Transiting Sun In The Second House**: During this period one's financial matters are highlighted. It is a time of receiving rewards, results, or financial gains from previous efforts initiated when the Sun transited through the first house. Hopefully there were efforts then. The most significant period in regards to monetary matters may happen within three days of the time this transit started, or when the Sun is within a one degree aspect of another solar return or natal planet while transiting this house.

**The Transiting Sun In The Third House**: During this period one tends to have many creative and inventive ideas. It favors sales, learning, speaking, writing, correspondence, and communications of all kinds. It is favorable in dealings with one's neighbors or siblings. It may also represent a time when the native might purchase an automobile or any communications devise. One may also consider reading a good book. The most significant time for creative ideas or successful communications endeavors may be within three days of the ingress into this house, or within one day of the transiting Sun making an aspect to a solar return or natal planet from within this house.

**The Transiting Sun In The Fourth House**: This is a period in which domestic and family matters assume greater importance. It favors quality time spent with one's family. It also favors time spent in contemplation or meditation, as an inner awareness seems to grow. Any transactions involving real estate or property may now be highlighted. Perhaps it is favorable for purchase of valuable home furnishings or appliances. It may also be a favorable time to

116

do something special with the family, even a vacation (which may also be in effect while the Sun transits the fifth house). Much of the family's attention may be centered upon the native.

**The Transiting Sun In The Fifth House**: Starting around this time one may commence a period of enjoyment, pleasure and fun. It tends to be favorable in relations with one's children, young people in general, and romance. Others may find the native attractive and a joy to be around. One may tend to be lighter and more vibrant than usual. All attention may be centered upon the native if he/she is in the public, and one seems to "shine" (and enjoy it). The most significant part of this time may be within three days of the ingress, or when the transiting Sun aspects another solar return or natal planet from this house.

**The Transiting Sun In The Sixth House**: This is a time when work duties are likely to predominate one's mind. The native may find him/herself working diligently on a specific project during this period, attending to great detail and/or analysis. There may be health concerns too. There may also be issues with co-workers that need to be worked out. Cooperation and compromise may be necessary. Overall, the quality of one's work is important, and as such, it may improve during this period.

**The Transiting Sun In The Seventh House**: During this period, emphasis will likely shift to partnerships, marriage, contracts and agreements. It is a period highlighting social engagements and meetings. One tends to be well-liked and popular, and attention may relax from the prior period's intensity of focus. Meeting people on their level may be beneficial. Offers and proposals may arise. Unions of many kinds tend to be positive. If the native is married, there seems to be an improvement either in relation with one's spouse, or his/her relations with other people. This may be a time to have meetings with one's agent, lawyer or accountant.

**The Transiting Sun In The Eighth House**: This begins a period which highlights finances - especially in agreements with others -

taxes, insurance, and possibly estate matters. If the native wishes to terminate or end a condition or relationship, now may be the best time to do so. This is favorable for research efforts if one is so inclined. There may be a conflict over money matters. This time favors any efforts for reform or "cleaning out" things one no longer needs. There may also be an increase in the native's sexual desires.

**The Transiting Sun In The Ninth House**: During this period one may have an opportunity to take a long trip, be involved in successful educational matters, or to teach. Generally speaking, it is a lighter time than the one just passed through. This period is given to expanding one's mind through philosophical discussions or readings. Dealings with people from foreign countries tends to be positive. Publishing ventures and legal matters tend to be successful now as well.

**The Transiting Sun In The Tenth House**: One's career is highlighted now. This is a period in which the native may "shine" professionally. One's status in the community, or within his/her profession, may increase. One could be held in higher regard, and his/her support may be sought by others. There native may glimpse his/her potential "destiny", of what one could do in this lifetime, and certainly within this year. It is a favorable time to handle responsibilities with skill.

**The Transiting Sun In The Eleventh House**: Rewards for professional efforts may be forthcoming during this period. This also highlights relationships with friends - a favorable time to engage in pleasurable or productive activities with friends. One may now pause to consider motivations for doing the things one is doing. "Am I engaged in group activities because of the glory I get from it, or because I believe in the principle or purpose of it?" An inner conflict might emerge temporarily, perhaps brought on through conversation with a friend, or a member of a group that the native is involved in. However, this period overall still indicates one has plenty of control and influence. There is an emphasis upon one's association with groups during this time.

118

**The Transiting Sun In The Twelfth House**: This is a period in which one may become more reclusive. Perhaps the native is beginning a project that requires great attention and freedom from distraction and interruptions. One may close off for from others for awhile. It favors research and projects which need time alone to complete. One's dreams may be very active, and goals may be very hazy - unclear. Physically the native may feel weaker than usual, so rest is important. Otherwise there may be illness or tiredness. This is a favorable time to offer help to others; they tend to benefit through the native's counsel.

# 12. CHAPTER TWELVE

# THE PROGRESSED SOLAR RETURN ANGLES

One of the most accurate techniques of timing significant events and changes during the year to a particular date is by progressing the angles of the solar return chart. The meridian (M.C. and I.C.) is progressed forward through the solar return chart at the same rate as the transiting Sun, or approximately one degree per day. In other words, if the Sun has transited 5 signs and 20 degrees from the time of the solar return, you may move the M.C. of the solar return forward 5 signs and 20 minutes to see where it is by progression. By the same token, you can then look up the corresponding Ascendant for that M.C. degree, and for the latitude of the city where the native was located at the time of the solar return, and that will represent the progressed horizon (Ascendant - Descendant axis) for that same day. Since calculating each of these dates may be time consuming, the reader may wish to consider using an astrological software program which will calculate these dates, like the Solar Return Program by the author, which is available through Seek-It Publications (publisher of this book).

The angles progressing through the solar return chart may be likened to transits: they "bring" conditions to the individual, according to the angle's nature. The planet receiving aspects by the progressed angle denotes either the type of person or event coming into the native's life, or the individual's likely response or expression to the event or person. The area of life emphasized is a combination of the angle involved (which is also an area of life), and the house which contains the planet being aspected, as well as the house which the planet rules in the solar return chart.

One point needs to be highlighted here: it is primarily the conjunction (or opposition) of the progressed angles to a solar return or natal planet that is important. Although other aspects, like the square and trine may coincide with events or conditions described by the angle and the nature of the planet(s) involved, it is primarily the conjunction/opposition aspect that consistently identifies times of the major events to which the return applies.

This technique of progressing the angles is reliable within a three-day time band, and usually within only one day. When used with the other techniques of prediction, like the progressed solar return Moon and the transits to the solar return chart, these dates can be an amazing indicator of significant events to unfold in one's life during this year. The following interpretations can serve as a guide for planning, or anticipating, certain events during the year based upon the passage of the progressed solar return angles over the natal and solar return planets:

**MC conjunct Sun**: A time of great success and recognition in one's work; growth or good news in one's vocation; increase of status; a good appearance in the public; confidence in one's work; a time of impressing others with successful efforts; favorable relations with men in the workplace; others looking to the native as a leader in the field, or community.

**IC conjunct Sun**: Success or recognition in one's family life; a favorable time for real estate transactions; happiness in family gatherings; favorable family activities; pride in one's family. This is a favorable time to have a gathering or to entertain in the home; a time to come into contact with a spiritual aspect of one's self; inner illumination; understanding brought on by quiet reflection.

**Asc conjunct Sun**: A time of great vitality and energy, when one might exude much confidence and psychological strength; a time of recognition and favorable attention; looking and feeling healthy; attractiveness to others who want to associate with the native; a creative time; a time of exhibiting leadership qualities.

121

**Des conjunct Sun**: This may be a time when others enter one's life who are attractive; one may be impressed, or positively affected, by others - and they may impressed with native as well; success with or for one's partner; a time to experience positive developments in marriage, partnerships, to sign contracts and make agreements; a time of popularity.

**MC conjunct Moon**: A time of changes in work; emotions may be high in regards to work; interesting or significant dealings with women at work; an opportunity to do something in the public; a time of combining work and family matters, perhaps real estate transactions; sensitivity in work or in regards to one's status; it may be a time of instability at work, or dealing with people who are over-emotional or dependent.

**IC conjunct Moon:** A time for closeness and intimacy in the home; an opportunity to relax with the family, or in quiet; real estate transactions may transpire; news from the family, or important developments affecting the family; attention is drawn to women in one's family - the wife or mother; the possibility of nurturing a special bond with someone the native loves, someone with whom there is a deep, mutual affection; emotional family issues or events.

**Asc conjunct Moon**: A time of many changes; the life may be in some sort of flux right now; difficulty seeing clearly due to highly charged emotions; the wish for security and stability, to get things completed and sorted out; changes in the home life or in regards to normal routines; significant developments involving women; it may be a time of intimacy and closeness, but one must be careful of becoming too dependent or emotional, except with those who are greatly trusted. This may be a favorable time to take a loved one out for the evening - dinner, entertainment, and/or romance.

**Des conjunct Moon**: A time of popularity and meeting people; favorable for social events and meeting people with whom one has an immediate bonding, as in a sense of already knowing them; meeting people with whom one feels comfortable; significant and emotional women in the life; changes within or regarding one's partnership(s); sensitivity to one's mate or partners, or awareness that they are more sensitive than usual; a favorable time to share something intimate; an unfavorable time to do something that hurts another; events which affect one's marriage and/or partnership.

**MC conjunct Mercury:** A time in which business matters may be highly emphasized; making deals; discussing ideas with business colleagues; speaking engagements - as a speaker or attendee; a learning opportunity that might benefit one professionally; a chance to work, to be of service at work; travel related to work, or communication with others from a distance; purchasing devises of communications to be used in work, i.e. computers, fax machine, telephone, etc.

**IC conjunct Mercury**: A time favoring communications and discussions in the home; a meeting in the home, or with family members; planning things to do with the home or family; purchasing communication devises to be used in the home (i.e. computers, fax machine, telephones, etc.); dealings with siblings or neighbors; discussing work plans in the home and with family members; negotiating a real estate or business transaction.

**Asc conjunct Mercury**: A time favoring communication and/or travel; there may be many new ideas one would like to express; favorable for writing, reading, speaking, or learning; a time of great intellect and mental alertness; good sense of humor; a time of making deals, and possible purchasing of things like computers, electronic devises, or communication objects; a favorable time to contact someone about an idea, or to receive a call from someone who has an interesting idea for the native to consider; favorable communication and possible proposals.

**Des conjunct Mercury**: A time of much communication and contact with others; many new ideas and thoughts being expressed and shared; major decisions involving others may be required, perhaps even signing of papers; a period in soliciting help from

123

others; meeting others who have interesting ideas to share; the meeting of intelligent or highly communicative people; a very busy time; being in contact with many people; agreements are highlighted, and so are work or service-oriented relationships.

**MC conjunct Venus**: A time which favors the culmination of an agreement; favorable experiences in relationships, both in work and in romance; support and appreciation for one's efforts; increase in business and income; successful completion of shared activities or goals; favorable developments in partnerships of any kind; working well with others; a decision made in one's favor.

**IC conjunct Venus**: A happy time in one's home or family; sharing a fond experience with members of the family, or with someone in the home; a successful gathering in the home (i.e. party); increased appreciation of the home or family (finding out the value of the home has increased); purchasing things of value for the home, or doing things of value with the family; love of one's home; love within one's home; compliments from others about one's home or family; a period favoring love and affection.

**Asc conjunct Venus**: A time in which the native's personal attraction is very high; one may look and feel very good; others are impressed with native; a time of charm and graciousness; favorable for being out in the public and being well-received; confidence and self-assuredness; financially this may be a successful time as others see value and worth in the native's efforts; a favorable time for meeting someone attractive; highlight on love.

**Des conjunct Venus**: A time when one is attracted to others; the emergence of someone interesting; making agreements; socializing and meeting people; giving and receiving support from others; a favorable time to be with others; happiness and success in partnerships or/marriage; highlight on love and romance; conducting activities that are favorably responded to by others.

**MC conjunct Mars**: A time of much activity and motivation in work; accomplishments through hard work; strategizing and making long-range plans; quarrels and arguments at work; upsetment caused by new conditions related to work; possibility of errors or mistakes; eager to attempt new things in regards to work or one's vocation; blazing a new trail and initiating new developments and/or products; highly motivated and busy period; a time of being upset with someone, probably in work.

**IC conjunct Mars**: A time of much activity in the home; highly motivated to do things in the home or in regard to the family; however there may be cause for anger in the home; a time of quarrels and disputes in the home; accidents in the home are now possible, so it is wise to be cautious and careful; a time in which one may hurt or offend those closest to native with harsh words; possibly being upset by family members or conditions.

**Asc conjunct Mars**: A time of great energy and drive, when one is highly motivated; a very active and possibly eventful time of the year; a time when one is likely to start new projects; a pioneering spirit, and a time of great independence and ingenuity; there may be a tendency towards arguments and anger now; it is wise to exercise great self-control and restraint; it is not wise to hurry or rush, as accidents may happen; a time of increased sexual passion.

**Des conjunct Mars**: A time of drawing very motivated and energetic - and perhaps competitive - people into one's life; meeting or knowing others who may be very angry, perhaps at native; meeting very domineering and self-centered people; a time of attraction, and perhaps wishing to enter into unions or agreements with others, but best to proceed slowly here; the possibility of a dispute, argument, or great upsetment, perhaps due to violations of agreements, or inconsiderate and insensitive actions by others towards the native or someone the native loves - and if so, the native may feel an urge to aggressively defend him/herself or another person; to fight for one's rights.

**MC conjunct Jupiter**: A time of favorable occurrences with regard to one's work; the successful implementation of a project, or culmination of a goal, and the resultant rewards and positive feedback from such well-done efforts; a "bonus" at work, or increased sales and/or income; opportunities to expand and grow at work; an offer, a proposal, that is flattering; the opportunity to enter into a professional agreement or contract; positive and successful meetings with others; successful judgments; a favorable time to make proposals; success socially and professionally; a travel (long-distance), teaching, or publishing opportunity; a time of "luck."

**IC conjunct Jupiter**: A time of great happiness and celebration in the home or with one's family; success in real estate ventures - buying and/or selling a home or property, or finding a place that one likes; perhaps an announcement of a birth, or marriage, or anniversary in the family; a favorable time to host a gathering or party in one's home amongst friends; a time of growth if engaged in any spiritual practice; an awakening that brings forth much inner joy; commencing a family vacation.

**Asc conjunct Jupiter**: A time of great happiness in general; a period in which one is likely to be very open-minded, charitable, optimistic, and of good cheer; enjoyment of activities with friends; a "good experience" with others; festive activities; success in one's social life as well as business; the opportunity to enter into agreements with others along the lines of one's interests; making proposals to others, and being accepted; a time of great joy and love of life; perhaps a time of too much drink, food, or indulgence in excess; a successful venture; entering into favorable unions with others through your own initiative; a "lucky" period, of winning contests.

**Des conjunct Jupiter:** A time of optimism regarding contracts, agreements, and activities involving others; receiving offers from others that are generous; the opportunity to enter into a partnership, or association, with another; great popularity with others, and demand for the native's time and presence; this may also be a time when others promise great things, but can they deliver on these promises? One would be wise to put these promises into a formal contract, and not rely heavily upon trust of what others say right now. In any event, contact with others seem very encouraging, and a source of excitement and happiness at this time. It is also favorable for any dealings with attorneys or agents - they may have something better than even the native conceived prior to meeting with them; this is a period of working well with others and coming to an agreement or understanding that is mutually beneficial; good fortune for one's partner(s).

**MC conjunct Saturn**: This is a time when one may experience disappointment, setbacks, or delays in attaining goals set for oneself; there may some disappointing news in regards to work; a time of rejections, denials, withholding of support that was desired; professional growth may be slowed; however it may be favorable for re-writing or re-stating or re-thinking one's goals more clearly now; the opportunity to organize thoughts and goals in regards to work; the potential of difficulties with parents or employers; tension or stress in one's work; the native may be best advised to take more time to work things out properly; not a favorable time to ask for favors or support at work; possible denial of one's requests.

**IC conjunct Saturn**: This is a time of disappointments, setbacks, or delays in regard to one's family or home life; tension in family relations; problems within the home (heating or air conditioning system, perhaps), possibly causing delays and inconvenience; setbacks possibly at work as well; a need to "get out" and escape worries; this time requires patience with oneself, and may be favorable for meditation or long-range planning, particularly regarding family matters; possibility of an illness in the family, or "coldness" with a family member, or someone living in your home.

**Asc conjunct Saturn**: This is a time in which one may feel "under the weather", stressed-out, pressured, and generally intense or serious; one may have a lot on the mind; tendency towards worry;

127

disappointments in either oneself or others may be present; it may be wise to have a task to do that does not have any time pressures attached with it; a favorable time for reading or studying, so long as there is no "test" associated with it; it is advisable to clear one's schedule at this time, for things may arise which prevent the native from fulfilling obligations satisfactorily; benefits may come from being disciplined and controlled; a time to accomplish something so long as distractions are avoided and one sticks to the schedule; lack of discipline may result in frustrations and falling behind in one's tasks; possibility of illness.

**Des conjunct Saturn:** This is generally not a favorable time for agreements or negotiations with others; others tend to resist the native, or in some way try to force one to "give in" to their demands, which are not always in the native's best interest; disappointment in others, especially if they exhibit a lack of integrity and willingness to follow through upon agreements already made; possibility of violating a contract or understanding, and letting someone else down, or being let down by another; tension in partnerships, marriage, or work associations; frustration in getting others to see one's point of view, or in general dealings with others; a rejection, or an effort to get one to accept "less"; a possibility of finally forging out a compromise and agreement, of putting it into form, but the native better check it carefully and be certain that it does not obligate beyond one's wishes; illness with one's mate or partner is possible; the mate or partner may be depressed and under much pressure, and may require the native's help or patience; on the other hand, the mate may not offer support which the native needs; a need to be sensitive to others, and to be around others who are supportive.

**MC conjunct Uranus**: This is a time when one is likely to experience sudden and unexpected events in regards to the profession; sudden changes at work or in responsibilities; the opportunity to start something new, or to end something suddenly (i.e. a job?); one tends not to get the response expected, and as a result, may be forced to make quick adjustments in plans, especially regarding work; a time of a sudden realization, which may be favorable in terms of understanding one's calling in life, but may be unfavorable if one fails to take it as a "sign"; the breaking of relations at work; the meeting of new people connected to work; being inspired with new ideas concerning one's work or calling in life; an incredible, enlivening experience, or a sharp disruption and interruption in one's plans, or both; a strong "sense of the future", and perhaps a psychic insight into something that will soon happen (i.e. prophetic thoughts).

**IC conjunct Uranus**: This is a time when one may experience a sudden jolt in the home or family life, as unexpected events arise; the possibility of electrical or computer failures in the home, or the possibility of purchasing a new computer or electronic devise in the home; a change in the home, for better or worse; it is favorable, perhaps, for trying to do something "modern" in the home (i.e. renovation); the advent of new people (strangers) entering the home, which if invited, could be highly stimulating; a sudden realization in one's spiritual path, an enlightening inner experience; a very creative and inventive time, one filled with much intuition and "sense of the future;" the potential of accidents and sudden interruptions in the home life, and possibly work life as well.

**Asc conjunct Uranus**: This is likely to be a time of great excitement, but also one of unexpected events arising in life; if flexible, this could become something quite positive, and certainly enlightening; a time of great inspiration, and perhaps willingness to take risks and try new things; a break from the normal pattern, and a tendency to act differently than others expect of the native; one may actually surprise, or shock others, with unexpected behavior; being unconventional, but highly interesting; magnetic, with the ability to attract new people into one's realm, but perhaps people with whom one shares very little in common, other than mental or physical "chemistry"; a "strange" personal experience may happen at this time; a tendency to feel very independent, and perhaps do things that are highly individualistic; this may not be a time of agreements with others, as they may not understand the native.

129

**Des conjunct Uranus**: This is a time when one may meet strange and unusual people; others may act very erratically, especially partners or mates; an unusual and unexpected experience with another person; agreements with others may be broken, and yet new agreements may be forged; difficulties with the mate or partner, or with an associate due to a possible misunderstanding, or intentional violation of an understanding; trying something new with a partner that is exciting; meeting new people with whom one may have little in common, yet the native is attracted to them, and they to the native; "strange" experiences to the partner.

**MC conjunct Neptune**: This is a time that is apt to be confusing in regards to one's work or reputation; misunderstandings over one's role - or the role of others - may cause hurt feelings; deception or even betrayal may be experienced at work or with others whom the native trusted; one's reputation may be vulnerable to attack; others may look up to the native, but perhaps they are putting him/her on a pedestal that sets them up for disappointment in the native, i.e. they had false expectations of the native, or the native of them; an undermining of one's goals by another is possible, who may even intentionally present the native in an incorrect and inaccurate light; dealings with "weasels"; this may be an excellent time for advertising or marketing projects, as one's imagination regarding work tasks is very stimulated; an experience with a "goddess;" a spiritual experience, and the feeling of great love or compassion for another; the possibility of being victimized by another, or truly helping or being helped by another (one may need to ask: "what is their motive?", for they may appear to offer help, but actually set the native up for betrayal).

**IC conjunct Neptune**: This is a time that may coincide with either very pleasant and beautiful experiences in the home, or great confusion; negatively there could be a tendency to be very absent-minded, forgetful of promises made to family members, intimate relations, or people in one's home; one may encounter deception or lies in the home, which can hurt; problems with insects, plumbing, roof, or water system are possible now - perhaps leaks caused from rains; positively this may a wonderful time of inner and spiritual experiences; it favors meditation; dreams may be very active; one may have an opportunity to truly help someone close by, perhaps a family member who is depressed, distraught, or confused; a sense of great compassion within the native is possible.

**Asc conjunct Neptune**: This is a time to be cautious of one's thoughts, as there may be a tendency towards fantasy and self-delusion; one may totally misunderstand something, or misread something, and if so, this may cause embarrassment; a tendency to be "in a fog", to not be totally in the here and now, to be forgetful and absent-minded; as one's imagination is highly stimulated, this may be a favorable time to entertain, to go out and have a romantic evening with someone the native loves (and trusts); it is not favorable in dealings with those whom one does not trust, or with whom one is suspicious; this is a time when one may need counseling or is able to provide counseling to others; it is a time of feeling vulnerable, and perhaps of being gullible; it is also a time in which one's body is highly sensitive to drugs, alcohol, or medications, and the immune system may be weak.

**Des conjunct Neptune**: This is a time in which one may be very vulnerable to impressions of others; others may not be what they appear, or do not represent what they claim, so the native is advised to proceed with caution in any negotiations and/or conversations; generally speaking this is not a favorable time to sign a contract, or come to an agreement - all the facts are not "on the table" yet; deception and deceit are possible if one is dealing with untrustworthy people - they are not likely to tell the native the truth, but rather hide important information; on the other hand, this may be a period of being attracted to glamorous events, of being with glamorous people; the attraction to very sensitive and romantic-minded individuals; meeting very imaginative and seductive people; this may be an excellent time to go out and entertain or dine with a mate, associate, or partner, especially if romantic intentions are on one's mind; the temptation to be infidel, or to be with someone who is infidel to another.

**MC conjunct Pluto**: This is a time when one may experience threats to their role at work; power plays and positioning for influence may cause much tension around the native; others may be plotting behind the native's back; the termination of a task or role or work; the need to change things as they are, perhaps forcibly, but hopefully with a sense of improving the condition; removal of a father-figure or a superior, or an experience of their intensity at work.

**IC conjunct Pluto**: This is a time in which one may encounter a very intense situation in the home or family; a time to be cautious of threats, or making threats to those close to the native as feelings could get very hurt; threat of damage to property; threat of illness in the family; the need for repair and healing in the home or family; the possibility of being undermined from someone close to the native; positively, this period favors research and deep study; a time of insight and discovery, particularly of oneself; a time of great psychological or spiritual understanding; an experience of personal power and/or strength.

**Asc conjunct Pluto**: This is a time of great intensity; one may feel obsessed, or driven with something or someone; it may be a time one seriously considers terminating a relationship - or something - from one's life; perhaps it is best to consider alternatives before drastic actions are implemented that hurt others or oneself is there any chance of a "win-win" in this situation? At its best, it is a time of deep insight, discovery, and positive influence over others; at its worse, it is a time of rage, of wanting to get even or destroy someone in some way; conflicts over money and/or power are possible now, in business or personal life; this may also be a time in which tax or insurance matters come up; it is a time requiring caution and avoidance of dangerous situations or feelings from within oneself; an act of coercion is possible, so avoid dealings with others who try to force one to do things against the will; on the same token, one is encouraged to avoid forcing others to do anything against their will.

**Des conjunct Pluto**: This is a time in which one may encounter others who try to force the native into accepting agreements or matters against one's will; a time of meeting very intense and forceful people; a period in which agreements and relationships may be terminated, or at least threatened with termination; conflicts over money or power with others; rejections from others is possible now; in all dealings with others, it is best to proceed slowly, and with the attitude of trying to find areas of compromise that benefit both parties - things can change for the better so long as it does not evolve into a contest over who has the power; positively, this may bring one in touch with very deep and profound people, or those who have done incredible research and who wish to share this with the native.

## 13. CHAPTER THIRTEEN

## KEEPING A DIARY OF YOUR SOLAR
## RETURN EXPERIENCE

Astrology is a language of symbols. It is also a study of time. At any given point in time, astrological symbolism is present which can assist in the understanding of that time.

Throughout one's life, people come in and situations arise. On the surface, these people are indeed people, and these situations are indeed specific, identifiable conditions. However, these people and these situations are also symbolic of lessons in life which each one of us are working on. Our experiences with these people and these conditions afford us an opportunity to understand ourselves more fully, to get a grasp on our patterns, and possibly to make a conscious effort to break those patterns if we so wish.

In the course of the solar return day, one will come into contact with different people and varying situations, One will experience certain conditions that arise in life. And one will react as well as interact with these people and circumstances. One will have impressions and make judgments concerning these events and interactions. In some cases, the individual will react favorably, and judge them as positive experiences. In other cases, that same individual may react more critically, and judge them less favorably.

The moments of these experiences and these interactions with others during the solar return day can be progressed into the future of this year. Basically the premise is this: whatever one experiences during the solar return day will symbolically represent the nature of that individual's experiences during the solar return year.

134

Furthermore, the time of these experiences - whether external or internal - will relate to a specific period in the year when that "symbolism" will likely repeat. The formula is the same as used in the calculation of the solar return Moon. That is, every two hours of time from the moment of the solar return represents one month of time from the date of that same solar return. In the same token, approximately every four minutes of time is the equivalent of one day in the solar return year.

Therefore it can be very enlightening to carry paper and pen with you on the day of your solar return. Mark down the time in which things happen during this day. In fact, you may want to keep a very detailed daily record of what happened as it goes along. It is also a good idea to plan things during the day which you know will be favorable and enjoyable, as that will set the tone for a favorable and enjoyable activity later on that year.

To briefly illustrate, let us assume your solar return occurs at 6:00 PM. At 8:00 PM, the circumstances that you experience (in the external world, or your interior world) will be symbolic of what is going on in your life about one month after your birthday. If you went out and had a wonderful dinner with someone you love, then perhaps one month later you will find your life very wonderful, almost like being out for a wonderful dining experience.

The daily record should begin six hours before your solar return, and continue 30 hours afterwards. The six hours before is symbolic of the three months leading up to your birthday. Even these events and circumstances are symbolic of what you have already gone through, and seeing the symbolism helps put the recent past into perspective. The six hours following the 24 hours of the birthday are also important. They refer to the momentum of this year carrying into the next solar return, and your ability to make the successful transition from one year's issues to the next.

# 14. CHAPTER FOURTEEN

## CHOOSING ONE'S SOLAR RETURN

One of the most exciting facts about solar returns is that you can actually choose your own horoscope wheel for the year! Your choice is limited, as might be expected, by both certain mundane as well as astrological factors. From an astrological point, your choice is limited to the angles and house placement of planets as well as rulerships, which covers quite a bit of territory. Your choice does not consist of what relationship (aspects) the planets will have to each other or to your other natal planets - only their relationship to your solar return angles and houses. From a mundane point of view, your choice is limited to your means and willingness to be mobile at the time of your solar return. The angles and houses are directly related to your location at the moment of your solar return; hence, your freedom and willingness to travel to a specific location will influence just how much choice you have in creating your own specially chosen horoscope for the year. And another limitation, of course, is your knowledge and ability to work with solar returns, for without this knowledge one has absolutely no choice in the matter whatsoever.

What you can determine, then, is the axes of the Earth - the horizon and meridian of the solar return chart. The actual moment of the solar return cannot be changed, but the local mean time (LMT) and consequently the True Sidereal Time of the solar return can be chosen; hence, the angles and houses - the "structure of the experience" in the forthcoming year - can also be chosen.

In choosing your solar return chart for any given year, there are two basic questions you might ask: first, "What area of life do I want to highlight (in a positive manner) this year?," and secondly, "What are my boundaries, or limitations, in traveling at the time of my solar return?" Obviously if the most astrologically desirable place to celebrate your solar return is somewhere in Libya, a combination of financial, governmental, and time factors, may make that choice an impossibility. So you must work within the boundaries of your means, or those means placed upon you by "outside" forces.

In answering the first question, you should remember some of the basic rules presented earlier. For instance, a balance of planets in the different house types is desirable; a majority of planets in angular houses - or at least three personal planets posited there - will indicate a "significant" year; an overabundance of planets in cadent houses will tend to indicate the opposite - a year of changes and/or preparation for future years.

Locating planets in harmonious aspect to an angle is most desirable, and so too is the positioning of benefics close to a house cusp - especially in that house which pertains to your areas of interest for this year. Another desirable placement is a harmonious aspect between a planet in a particular house to the planet which rules that house. If you are able to arrange for a combination of these factors to occur, according to the house chosen to be highlighted, then it is a favorable indication that matters ruling that area of your life will flow successfully in the coming year.

There are of course some factors that will inhibit even the finest of house and angle arrangements. If the aspects between your solar return planets to each other, and even to your natal planets, are discordant according to the expressions you wish to highlight, there is not much that can be done to "assure" their favorable expression this year. At best, the you can "lessen" their potential negative manifestation by traveling somewhere that will position an angle to make a "soft" (harmonious) aspect to one of the planets involved. For example, if there is a T-Square in the solar return chart involving planets in houses that you have determined are important to you in the coming year, then you may wish to travel somewhere at the time of your solar return that will bring the horizon (Ascendant - Descendant axis) or meridian (Midheaven and I.C. axis) into a favorable aspect (sextile/trine) to the planet and/or house ruler you are concerned about.

It is also possible to more greatly empower positive aspects between planets in your solar return chart by simply traveling to a point in which these same angles make yet another positive aspect to them. For instance, if you have a trine between two planets that relate to an area of great personal interest this year, you might consider traveling somewhere for your birthday that will find the Midheaven or Ascendant forming a grand trine to these planets. That location would greatly enhance the expression and experience of the two trining planets during the course of the year.

If you are not an astrologer, and you are interested in designing a solar return chart that most positively highlights your solar return planets, you are advised to consult a well-trained, qualified and professional astrologer who can assist you in this matter. This would be greatly suggested in the event that you find certain parts in the "Planets In Aspect To Angles", or "Planets Conjunct The Solar Return House Cusps" sections of particular concern. Those conditions can be altered simply by traveling for your solar return. In addition, planning a trip on your birthday is an excellent idea. It will cause you to put great conscious effort into that most sacred of all days of the year for you personally - your birthday, the day the Sun and Earth return to their exact position of your birth moment. It is a special day for you every year. Treat it with reverence. Make its unfoldment an annual pilgrimage, a mission, a challenge for you to have a super experience. The experiences of that day will be the foundation for the whole of your next year of life.

# CHAPTER 15

## PUTTING IT ALL TOGETHER:
## CASE HISTORIES FROM THE PERSONAL
## FILE

One of the great joys in being an Astrologer has been acting as a "cosmic travel agent" for clients who have been willing to travel for their solar return. Listening to the recaps of their adventures, and how the "one degree per day angular progression method" has accurately pinpointed specific events during the course of their year, has been an experience of continuous amazement.

I remember one year in which I received a telephone call - on my business line - for my wife at 8:00 AM in the morning. First of all, my wife doesn't receive personal calls on my business line. Second, no one calls me at 8:00 AM in the morning, except traders around the world (part of my consulting business is for futures traders, particularly early in the morning). But this lady sounded very determined: she wanted to speak to Mrs. Merriman, and she said this with a very confident and cheerful voice. So I went to get my wife, who was doing her normal early morning shower. When I informed her she had a phone call on my business phone, she shouted back: "Tell them I am in the shower and will call them back." To which I replied: "I think you should take this call now." I don't know why I insisted she take it now - something in my gut said she should, and long ago I learned to trust these feelings.

So she did. She reluctantly stepped out of the shower, wrapped a towel around her lovely figure, and took the cordless phone I handed her. A moment later, she was screaming with joy.

"What happened?" I asked. I couldn't stand the mystery. Who was this woman who called my wife at 8:00 AM on my phone, and caused my wife to scream with happiness? If only I could do the same.....

"That was the radio station W???. I just won $100.00!" And to think: if I hadn't trusted my gut instinct, I would have told this person to call back later and my wife would not have won this prize.

Now comes the second part of the mystery. Why now? What was going on in my wife's chart that would indicate she would win $100.00 today? I looked up her progressions. Nothing. I looked up transits to her natal planets. Nothing regarding "luck."

"Aha," I thought. It must be in her solar return chart. Maybe even her "progressed solar return angles" hitting a natal or solar return planet. I quickly ran up the Matrix version of the Solar Return Report Writer, and did a print-out of the "one-degree per day progressed angles" for the year. Sure enough, there it was: the progressed solar return ascendant was exactly conjunct her solar return Jupiter that very day. The print out read: "A time of great joy... a 'lucky' period, of winning contests."

By the way, that progressed ascendant would not have hit that Jupiter that day if the "residence", or "birth place" location was used. It only applied for the chart that was in effect based upon where she was physically located for her solar return. Every year my wife and I travel for our solar returns to create a chart - with certain planetary/angular relationships - of choice.

Later that same year I had an opportunity to lecture in Ghent, Belgium. On the morning of the lecture, I had a meeting with the sponsor, who published a very successful astrological magazine. He was very interested in both markets and astrology. He was particularly interested in the Solar Return Report Writer software program, and wanted to see a demonstration of it.

140

As the report was printing out, I explained to him the fact that it would identify and interpret 76 potentially important dates during the year in which this "one degree per day angular progression method" would conjunct each solar return and natal planet. On this particular day, it showed the progressed I.C. of his current solar return chart was conjuncting his Uranus. "You see," I said, "you are hosting an astrological gathering tonight, and Uranus is being conjunct by one of these angles today." After all, Uranus rules both astrology and group gatherings. I thought the chart was sufficiently speaking to the matter at hand. However, my host had a far more serious look on his face as he read the text for this progressed IC conjuncting his Uranus this day. Right at the beginning of the interpretation, it stated: "... the possibility of electrical or computer failures in the home, business, or work setting." Just an hour before our meeting, his computer (in his home) had "crashed." He had just lost all his data.

These are just a couple of the numerous examples of how the unique methods employed in this book work. But let's take a look at how one might apply these concepts and with this knowledge, create a solar return horoscope that compliments the goals one might set for him/herself for a particular year. I will be using my own life experiences to demonstrate these techniques, thereby not risking a breech of confidentiality regarding my clients. In other words, I am giving myself permission to put into print personal experiences that may be helpful in understanding how the reader might prepare and commence a solar return.

**Cases 1 and 2:** In 1977 my wife and I had just married. We took out a rental apartment in the very nice community of Rochester, Michigan. This was close to Birmingham, Michigan, which is where my wife had spent all of her life, and close to where I had spent a good deal of my own life. We were young and she had Venus in Cancer natally, so it didn't surprise me that just a couple of months after our marriage - when thinking of what she would like to highlight for her July, 1977 solar return - she stated: "I want to buy our own home." It didn't matter that we had spent all our money to

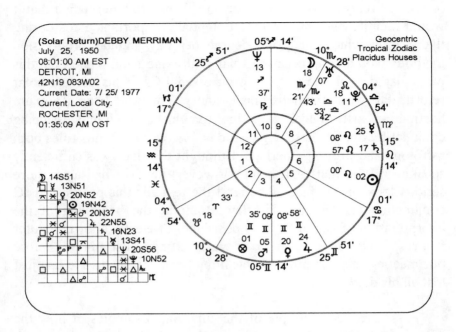

**Figure 8: 1977 solar return for Rochester, MI, place of residence.**

have a great wedding party on May 18, 1977. She was a woman of
unlimited faith in my ability as an astrologer. If she wanted a home,
she knew that I could create the type of solar return chart that
would grant this wish (did I mention that she had Mars conjunct
Neptune in the second house and Jupiter in her natal seventh?).
Being the magician I was in 1977, I granted her wish. Well, I
calculated a location at the time of her 1977 solar return that would
highlight this possibility. Being a double Capricorn myself, I can tell
you quite honestly that I had more than a little doubt about this
wish coming true in spite of the fact that the solar return chart
would support such a possibility.

She wanted a house. Her own (our own) house. "Well," I
thought, "we better highlight the fourth house with benefics, or
place the Moon prominent in this chart." The fourth house
represents one's home, as does the Moon.

142

The first step was to draw up a solar return chart for her residence. Why travel if you don't have to for a solar return? The chart for her 1977 solar return in Rochester, Michigan is shown in Figure 8. Right away I noticed that Mars was conjunct the IC, Saturn was conjunct the Descendant and square to the Moon. Right away I didn't like what I was seeing. Two malefics - Mars and Saturn - conjunct the two angles. One angle ruled the home (Mars, IC), and the other ruled her marriage (Saturn, Descendant). I also noticed two benefics - Venus and Jupiter - were in the fourth house, and in wide trine to the Ascendant. This later configuration supported the possibility of getting a new home, but the other two - especially the Moon square Saturn, and Saturn on an angle - did not. In fact, it looked more like her knight in shining armor (me) was about to become tarnished because he could not produce the magical new home. "Arrrghhhh," I screamed. "Let's get out of here for your birthday." Debby was never one to refuse a summer vacation to a new and exciting location. After all, she was a Leo with the Moon in Sagittarius trine her Mercury. She loved to travel.

I saw two things that had to be done to modify this chart more into alignment with the realization of her goals. The first was to break up this Moon/Saturn square, which was highlighted by the fact that Saturn was conjunct an angle. It would be better - for the realization her goals - to get that Saturn in a trine to the M.C. (Midheaven). Second, the possibility of a new home would be enhanced if that Venus conjunct Jupiter could be put into an orb of conjunction to the IC, which is the home. The fact that Mercury ruled the IC and formed a favorable trine the Venus/Jupiter conjunction was also supportive. Of course this meant putting Mars back into the third house, and as I explained to Debby, "This means we are sacrificing your brother for the sake of our marriage and your wish for a home." She saw no problem with that trade-off. Who was I to argue?

Through trial and error (we didn't have computer programs to help us with re-location back then), I calculated Machias, Maine as the ideal place to travel to for her 1977 birthday. The chart for this

143

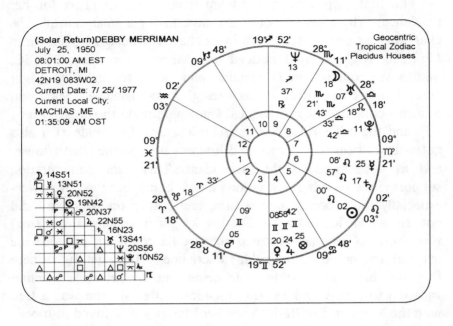

**Figure 9: 1977 solar return for Machias, Maine**

solar return is shown in Figure 9. This re-located solar return dropped Saturn from the 7th house cusp down into the 6th house, but now it formed a favorable trine to the newly constructed M.C. It thereby broke up that worrisome Moon square Saturn aspect. Furthermore Machias, Maine placed the solar return Venus less than half a degree off the IC, and of course it still formed a conjunction to Jupiter, and both formed a sextile to the Saturn and Mercury, the later which ruled the 4th house of one's home. The sacrifice was putting Mars in the third house and in wide square to the Ascendant, and Neptune in the same wide aspect but from the ninth house. I felt this was an acceptable compromise - seldom is everything perfect - for the other modifications complimented her wishes for her new year. So, in late July of 1977, my wife, my daughter, and I loaded up the car and began a journey to the far corner of Maine, where the state butts up against New Brunswick on the Canadian border.

144

Note that her solar return for this year would take place one day before her actual birthday. Her actual birthday is July 25, but in this year, her solar return would occur at 9:34 PM, Eastern Daylight Time, on July 24. Our goal was to arrive in the area six hours early, and stay at least another 30 hours, within 60 miles of Machias.

We arrived in plenty of time at the home of famed Astrologer Francis Sakoian and her husband Sark. The Sakoians had been friends of ours for several years, and we always enjoyed opportunities to be with them at their summer home in the bustling artistic community of Bar Harbor, Maine - about 50 miles west of Machias. On the morning of Debby's solar return, we drove up to Saint Stephens in New Brunswick, a beautiful little city in neighboring Canada. Later that afternoon we drove back down to the quiet village of Machias where we came upon one of those famous New England lobster diners. The three of us enjoyed a great lobster dinner, then drove to quiet spot for Debby to meditate as her solar return unfolded. The following 30 hours were comprised of a drive back to the Sakoians, a good night's rest, and the next day of doing all the things that Debby would enjoy - climbing the mountains of Bar Harbor, shopping in the arty stores of this vibrant city, and socializing with our very friendly host and hostess. As always, we try to do our best to make sure the birth day person has a "dream come true" type of a day.

This, then, completed Debby's solar return period for 1977. Her goal for this year was to purchase a home. But, as I told her, "Don't expect it until the Sun transits her solar return IC, Venus and Jupiter." Since they were in Gemini and she was a Leo, this would give me slightly more than ten months to figure out a way to make that much money.

Case #2 involves my chart for this same period. I was newly wed, madly in love with my new bride. The most important thing to me was to make her happy. And now she wanted a new home, and I wasn't exactly rich. My birthday was - is - exactly five months after hers, or December 25. So the goal for my birthday

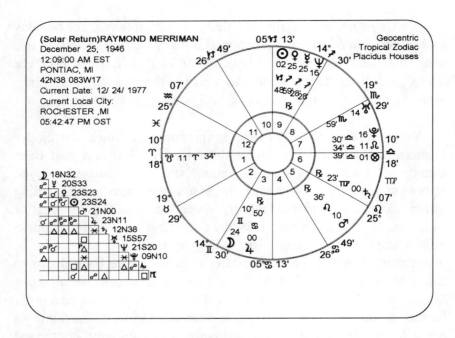

**Figure 10: Author's solar return for 1977, residence.**

would be - guess what? - a new home. A secondary goal however would have to be to do well in my practice so I could afford this new home.

Once again, the first step was to draw up a solar return chart for the place of residence, or Rochester, Michigan. This chart is shown in Figure 10 at the top of this page.

This chart wasn't too bad. It had Aries rising, with Mars in the fifth house trining the Ascendant, and the Moon's North Node conjunct the Descendant. Saturn was in early Virgo, in a wide trine to both the Sun and the M.C., and ruling both. However, the vast majority of planets were in cadent houses, which denoted a potential year of insignificance. The Aries rising might have mitigated that somewhat, but it would potentially be a more noteworthy year if I could find a place that would move more planets into angular houses.

146

In the chart of this day, one can observe that the Sun was in opposition to Jupiter, and both were close by (on cadent side) to the meridian angles (M.C. and IC respectively). Furthermore, the Moon was in an "out-of-sign" conjunction to Jupiter, and ruled the fourth house cusp, which favored getting a home if it could be placed angular.

Through trial and error, the location of Lake Geneva, Wisconsin was chosen as optimizing the astrological factors which I believed were consistent with my goals for the new year. By traveling to Lake Geneva for Christmas, 1977, I would create a chart with the first degree of Aries rising, which would represent a new beginning. It would also move Jupiter to conjoin the IC, and place Saturn in an exact trine to M.C., which it ruled. It would move the Sun into the tenth house, and only two degrees removed from the M.C., which would portend success in my career. Jupiter on the IC would of course support the vision of moving into my own home, or at least a happy family dynamic. This chart is shown in Figure 11, on the top of the next page.

The time of this solar return would be 11:42 AM, Central Standard Time, on December 24, 1977. Being born on Christmas day, and having one's solar return always right around Christmas, has its drawbacks if you have family. However being an astrologer has many privileges too, and in this case, I was about to receive just such a good fortune that comes from being in this profession. Another famous Astrologer and good friend Carol Rushman just so happened to own a condominium in Lake Geneva, Wisconsin. And, as fate often works out for someone born with Venus conjunct Jupiter, she wasn't using it this particular Christmas. "Ray," she said, "if you want to fly in and pick up the key, it's yours for your solar return." Carol, you see, also happens to recognize the importance of traveling to the "best" place for one's solar return. So off I went to Wisconsin, land of milk, cheese, and Lake Geneva. The village by the way was - is - very beautiful, situated right on a lovely lake of the same name.

147

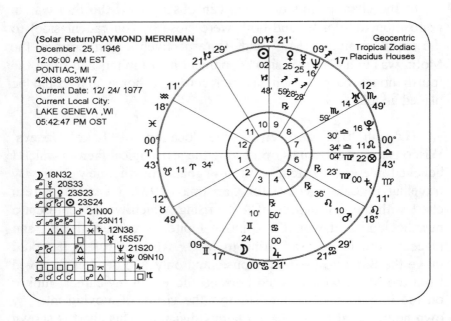

**Figure 11: Author's relocated 1977 solar return to Lake Geneva, Wisconsin**

The chart above was chosen to enhance the purchase of my first home, and the success of my vocation. During the year, I published my first two books on Astrology. One was *Evolutionary Astrology: The Journey of the Soul Through The Horoscope*, and the first edition of this book, *The Solar Return Book of Prediction*. I formed my own publishing house, and called it Seek-It Publications. Each of these endeavors succeeded beyond my wildest dreams.

By June of 1978, as the Sun entered Gemini, I had earned enough money to afford a new house. As the Sun approached 19 degrees of Gemini, conjunct Debby's solar return IC, Jupiter and Venus, and near my solar return Moon, we decided to go out house-looking. Debby wanted to move to Birmingham, where she lived most of her life, and I wanted to move out into the country near Clarkston, Michigan, near where I grew up. So on a bright, sunny day in June, she made an appointment with a realtor to look

148

at homes in Birmingham, while I made an appointment to look at acreage in the Clarkston area with yet a different real estate agent. That night we both returned with a look of great discovery in our faces. "I found the perfect house," exclaimed Debby. To which I replied, "I found the perfect land to build a new home on 13+ acres near Clarkston!."

What to do? Well, her IC, Venus, and Jupiter were in Gemini, and so was my solar return Moon. We made a bid on the Birmingham house the day the Sun hit 24 of Gemini (her solar return Jupiter and my Moon). The bid was accepted. One week later, and my solar rerun M.C. progressed over my solar return IC and Jupiter, our bid on the 13+ acre property was also accepted. We bought both! And we bought both on days that related to the re-located solar return charts - not the residence or birth place-located charts.

But something else also happened that year that did not show up in the residence or birth place charts, but only the solar return charts. Her brother had a car accident (remember, we moved Mars from the fourth into the third house, square the Ascendant?). He recovered - after all, Venus and Jupiter were conjunct her fourth house cusp of family relations. Everyone in the family was happy. And I was still a wonderful knight in shining armor to my new wife (Sun conjunct M.C.).

**Case #3:** In many respects, a properly planned solar return experience is akin to being the ultimate Feng Shui of astrology. As with Feng Shui, the practitioner of solar returns must take into account the *intentions* of the subject, and then perform the art of *arrangement* concerning the setting and location. In the case of solar returns, the *intention* has to do with the client's goals for the year, if not for the entirety of one's life. In other words, goals for the year are most attainable when they are consistent with the overall view of one's entire life. The *arrangement* serves the purpose of enhancing the attainment of those goals, the realization of one's visions, and a behavior consistent with one's values and highest attitudes. This is reflected in the arrangement of one's planets in a horoscope (solar return horoscope) that the astrologer chooses. Thus the solar return consultant calculates a location for the time of one's solar return that will *reflect* - show an arrangement of - planets in houses and planets in aspects to angles that are in alignment with that client's intentions, goals, vision, values, and desired attitudes for this period of his/her life (i.e. the year pertaining to the solar return). The *arrangement* is further augmented by the actual efforts the native puts forth into that sacred event- what he/she does during that solar return period.

The first step, then, is to determine the individual's *intentions* for the year. On December 25, 1996, the author (me) would be celebrating his 50th year of existence in this incarnation. Age 50 is a significant milestone in anyone's life. It is half a century. It has the ring of being a halfway point of one's lifetime - at least one's adult lifetime. It is a point where he is liable to cross the line between being young and energetic to becoming an "old fart." As such, it is cause for significant reflection and re-evaluation of everything one has done in the life up until that point. "Have I accomplished to my potential? Am I happy with what I have done in my life? Do I have any regrets? Are there things I wish I would have done differently? What would I like to do with the *rest of my life* now?" These are the questions that goes through one's mind at age 50 - the very questions that we as astrologers expect to go through under Saturn returns. Of course, this particular solar return in 1996 found Saturn square my natal Sun, and just beginning its sojourn above my natal horizon after spending the 14 years below it. But back to the purpose of this chapter, which is learning the art of astrological arrangement via solar returns.

In choosing a location for my 50th solar return, it was necessary to begin by understanding my *intention* at this point in my life. My *intention* was to experience a profound level of gratitude, of thankfulness, for my life experience up until this point. After several long periods of contemplation, I realized that I was most thankful for what I called: "Astrology and the three F's:

150

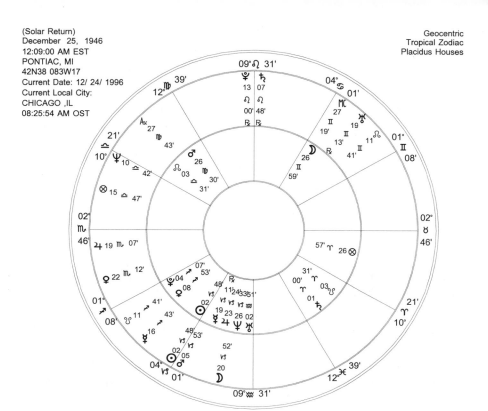

(Solar Return)
December 25, 1946
12:09:00 AM EST
PONTIAC, MI
42N38 083W17
Current Date: 12/ 24/ 1996
Current Local City:
CHICAGO ,IL
08:25:54 AM OST

Geocentric
Tropical Zodiac
Placidus Houses

**Figure 12: Author's solar return for 1996, relocated for Chicago.**

Family, Friends, and Financials." These four areas defined the most important values of the life I had lived so far, and I was deeply thankful for each.

Thus the initial step was to find a suitable location that would reflect these areas, and this profound feeling of gratitude I was experiencing. The next step would then consist of creating an experience around that time - and in that location - that would also reflect these same intense values and feelings.

The location chosen for the 1996 solar return - with these intentions in mind - was Chicago, Illinois. The chart is shown in Figure 12. This location was particularly hard to choose because of some very strong planetary aspects in effect. For instance, Saturn was square to the most important planet in the chart - the Sun. The

151

Moon is also quite important, and was in a tight square to Mars. What made this last aspect so significant, though, was the fact that the Moon would be within minutes of my natal MC, and Mars just slightly more than 1 degree off my Ascendant. Venus and Pluto were also conjunct for this year, which probably related to the intensity of thankfulness I was experiencing.

The first task, I believed, was to *arrange* the angles in a manner that would highlight the Sun favorably. The Sun squared Saturn, I was making the turn at a symbolic halfway point in life, and rather than "feel old and like giving up", I wanted to feel productive and healthy. Choosing Chicago would create a horoscope with 2°54'♏ rising. It would form a nearly exact sextile to my Sun, which would fall in the second house, close to the cusp of the third. This favored another goal I had for the year, which was to complete a book on *Stock Market Timing* that I had started a year earlier. Furthermore, any favorable aspect from the Sun to the Ascendant is conducive to good health and physical stamina, which were other goals I valued.

Chicago would also produce a 9°♌ Midheaven. This concerned me a bit because my natal Saturn and Pluto were at 7 and 13 degrees of Leo respectively, thus conjuncting this re-located MC. In Farmington Hills, my residence, the MC would have been 13°♌, exactly conjunct my natal Pluto. However, as one can see in the chart shown in Figure 12, the solar return Venus was almost at 9 degrees of Sagittarius, within one degree of an exact trine to this re-located MC. Since the solar return Venus was conjunct the solar return Pluto, the re-located MC would favorably highlight this aspect. The fact that the Venus/Pluto conjunction fell in the solar return second house of finances brought into play one of my three "F's" for the year - financials. The fact that this MC conjunct my natal Saturn and Pluto, which were in my natal 11th house and both were now trined by the solar return Venus/Pluto, highlighted the value (second house, Venus) I placed upon long-term (Saturn) friendships (11th house).

The area of friendships was furthermore heightened by the placement of my natal Ascendant (27 Virgo), and solar return Mars and North Node, in the solar return 11th house of friendships. Mars formed a trine to Neptune, which was located in the third house as part of a stellium involving Mercury, Jupiter, and Uranus. Mercury ruled this 11th house, and Jupiter as well as Uranus are planets pertaining to one's friends.

The area of family values would be highlighted in the chart no matter what location was chosen. The solar return Moon (family) was conjunct the natal MC (peak life experience, life purpose), and the natal Moon (family) was conjunct the solar return Mercury (communication) and Jupiter (kindness, thankfulness). There was concern about this solar return's IC being Aquarius, and its ruler Uranus forming a square to the Ascendant, and the solar return Moon was squared by Mars. However it was believed that the aforementioned supportive aspects would balance - and even tip towards "favorable" - this area of life.

Highlighting the area of Astrology would prove to be a complex task. What really rules Astrology? Many astrologers believe the planet Uranus rules this study. But actually it depends more upon how the astrologer one wishes to apply Astrology that is important. In my case, I wanted to do an intense, deep study on a specific aspect of Astrology - specifically Stock Market Astrology - that would result in the publication of a major book on the subject. In other words, I wanted to do tireless and exhausting research, followed by writing on the results of this study. For this approach to Astrology, this chart would appear to be very favorable. The Scorpio rising would lend intensity to research efforts. It's ruler - Pluto - was trine to the MC. The third house of writing was loaded with benefics and planets conducive to this task. Mercury and Jupiter were conjunct, which favored both writing and publishing. Furthermore, both were conjunct by the natal Moon, and trine to both the solar return Mars and natal Ascendant. This was all supportive of creativity and productivity in intellectual or mental pursuits.

153

This, then, completed the Feng Shui of arranging the proper horoscope for a solar return. This chart would support the *intentions* of the subject, which was myself.

The next step was to produce the physical setting - create the experience - that would symbolically reflect these same intentions. We knew *where* the solar return would be - Chicago. But now we had to create a ritual that would both symbolize and empower the goals of the individual - which in this case had to do with intense gratitude and thankfulness for Astrology, Family, Friends, and Financials. For this, a special "celebration" was planned by the author's oldest daughter, who is (at this time) a lawyer residing in Chicago. She asked for a guest list of about 20 people to invite to a dinner and after-dinner entertainment.

A guest list was formed of two astrologers (and their families), two major friends of the native (me), two people in the field of financials in the area of Chicago, and all the author's immediate family (wife and children). Barbara Schermer (and her husband Robert Craft) of Chicago was one of the astrologers present (the other was Jeff Jawer and his family, who at the time were living near Big Rapids, Michigan). Barb chose the restaurant for the gathering. It was *Widow Newton's* on the Navy Pier. This restaurant was owned and operated by one of Barbara's clients, and actually had an astrological motif. A special invitation was written by the author's very good friend Robert June of Michigan, who also attended, and then designed by the author's wife, Debra. Aimee (the lawyer daughter) then sent out 20 invitations, and coordinated the entire evening.

Thus the Feng Shui of the actual experience was arranged properly. The location chosen was Chicago because it created the proper chart. The author's intentions had to do with Astrology, Family, Friends, and Financials - and representatives (symbols) of each of these areas of the author's gratitude were present. As might be expected, the evening was a beautiful and memorable experience.

After the dinner, the party moved from *Widow Newton's* restaurant back to Barb and Bob's house, where it lasted until midnight. From there, about five of the group went to a downtown Chicago Blues Club, danced and enjoyed the music until 2:00 AM. Shortly after, all parties returned to the hotel. The subject (me) then went into meditation as the precise moment of the solar return unfolded at 2:26 AM. The next day, a series of planned enjoyable activities by the native (me) was initiated, including shopping, giving of gifts, going to the movie "Shine" (which was about a concert pianist who went mad and was "saved" by an astrologer he ended up marrying), and doing one taped consultation for pay (the author always tries to do one taped consultation for pay during the 24 hours following his solar return, as it symbolizes "making money for the year").

As the year unfolded, all areas of the author's intentions came to realization. The most significant developments of the year following this solar return were: the completion of the first volume of *The Ultimate Stock Market Timing Book: Cycles and Patterns in the Indexes*; the formation of a wonderful new friendship with Dutch astrologer Joyce Hoen; co-organizing the marvelous ARC international astrological conference on "The Cosmic Experience" at Michigan State University; teaching an astrology class for the first time to fantastic group of professional astrologers in Basel, Switzerland; and visiting the Burgogne wine region of central France with good friend and astrologer Jeffe Anders. On retrospect, I can look back upon this year and realize that, truly, life is good, and my life in particular is blessed with good friends, good family, and good business relations (both in the field of Astrology and Financials). Like the fine wines of the Burgogne, life in my 50th year was full-bodied and satisfying.

**Case Example #4**: The only thing not covered so far in the afore-mentioned case studies is the symbolism of events that occur during the 36-hour period surrounding the solar return. That is, what happens six hours prior to the solar return, and 30 hours afterwards, has a symbolic correlation to what happens three months prior to the birthdate, through the next birth year, and the the months following that birth year.

As described in a prior chapter, the 24-hours following the moment of one's solar return symbolize themes that are likely to be present during the following 12 months (i.e. the solar return year). Additionally, the six hours prior to the solar return correlate to themes present three months prior to the solar return birth date, and the six hours following the 24-hour period still carry over into the first three months of the following solar return. Thus 24 hours following the solar return moment equates to the following 12 months of life. Or, every two hours equates to one month, and every 4 minutes equates to one day. Thus the six hours before the return moment represent the three months prior to the birth date, and the 30 hours afterwards correspond to the 15 months which are to follow the birth date.

To show how this works, let's examine the author's 1997 solar return experience.

The location chosen for the author's 51st solar return was Tucson, Arizona (see Figure 13). The reason for choosing this solar return location should be obvious by now. It put the Sun right on the solar return Ascendant, and Jupiter in the second house, in exact trine to the solar return MC. Once again the author was blessed with good friends in astrology who helped bring in this cycle. Noted astrologers Susie Cox of Tucson, and Erin Sullivan of Phoenix hosted a small celebration which also included friend and financial markets colleague Robert Miner of Dynamic Traders' Inc. in Tucson.

The actual time of the solar return event for Tucson occurred at 7:24 AM, December 24, 1997. Six hours prior to this moment I had returned from the gathering of friends to the beautiful Westward Look Resort where my wife was waiting up for me, and my two youngest children were fast asleep. Without going into detail, let me just say that my wife proceeded to present me with a birthday

156

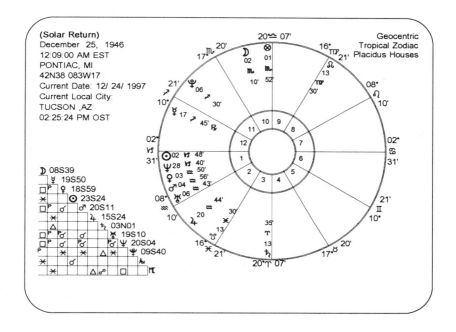

**Figure 13: Author's 1997 solar return, relocated for Tucson, Arizona.**

gift of the most intimate kind - a very good way to celebrate one's solar return experience. I then went to sleep very contentedly, entering into a world of wonderful dreams, and thinking about my goals for the next year.

I woke up just before the moment of the solar return, and quickly went off by myself to say a prayer. I had a full day of activities planned, including a massage, chiropractic adjustment, visit to the fabulous Canyon Ranch Resort and Spa, and then back to Phoenix for the night prior to boarding an early Christmas morning flight back to home.

The following grid depicts the times and the events that occurred during the 1997 solar return experience. It also denotes the times during the year in which themes of a similar nature would

157

be likely to unfold, based upon the theory that every two hours of time represents 1 month of the life, and every 4 minutes of time represents one day of life. Remember: The solar return occurred at 7:24 AM. Every four minutes before represents one day prior to December 24, 1997, and every four minutes afterwards pertains to a symbolism of every day afterwards.

| Time of Day | Calendar Correspondence | Event or Experience |
|---|---|---|
| **12/24/97** | | |
| 1:00 - 1:30 AM | 9/18-9/26, 1997 | Intimacy with wife. |
| 1:30 - 7:15 AM | 9/26-12/22 | Peaceful sleep |
| 7:15 - 7:45 AM | 12/22-12/29 | Prayer and quiet |
| 7:45 - 8:00 AM | 12/29/97 - 1/2/98 | Bathroom daily preparations |
| 8:00 - 8:30 AM | 1/2 -1/10 | Breakfast served - and eaten |
| 8:30 - 9:15 AM | 1/10 - 1/22 | Kids upset about not being home |
| 9:15 - 10:05 AM | 1/22 - 2/4 | Drive to Message and Chiropractor Mood is somber as we will split up |
| 10:05 - 10:40 AM | 2/4 - 2/13 | Excellent body work treatment |
| 10:40 - 11:00 AM | 2/13 - 2/18 | Susie Cox arrives; drive to Canyon Ranch Resort and Spa |
| 11:00 - 2:00 PM | 2/18 - 4/3 | Feel great! Great workout and Spa experience! |
| 2:00 - 2:25 PM: | 4/3 - 4/9 | Drive back to Susie's house |
| 2:25 - 3:15 PM: | 4/9 - 4/22 | Missed Debby and had to wait, but we got to spend time talking with Erin. |
| 3:15 - 3:30 PM: | 4/22 - 4/26 | Debby and kids arrive; good-byes and thank yous to Susie and Erin. |
| 3:30 - 6:00 PM: | 4/26 - 6/3 | Drive from Tucson to Phoenix - went well. |
| 4:00 - 5:00 PM: | 5/3 - 5/18 | Did a taped consultation for pay. |
| 6:00 - 6:30 PM: | 6/3 - 6/11 | Got off on the wrong exit in Phoenix, but it took us through a scenic area - great sunset. |
| 6:30 - 7:40 PM: | 6/11 - 30 | Settled in hotel and dressed up for dinner. |
| 7:40 - 8:00 PM: | 6/30 - 7/4 | Nice drive to Camelback Inn for dinner |

| | | |
|---|---|---|
| 8:00 - 10:00 PM: | 7/4- 8/3 | Wonderful Christmas Eve dinner at the Camelback Inn and Resort. |
| 10:00 - 11:00 PM | 8/3 - 8/18 | Return to hotel and electricity goes off. We light candles and open gifts. It is very nice. |
| 11:00 - 12:01 AM | 8/18 - 9/3 | We pack luggage and go to bed. |

**12/25/97**

| | | |
|---|---|---|
| 12:01 - 6:00 AM: | 9/3 - 12/3 | Sleep, excited about going home for Christmas. |
| 6:00 - 6:30 AM: | 12/3 - 12/11 | Wake up and go. |
| 6:30 - 7:00 AM: | 12/11 - 12/19 | Check out and drive to airport - excitement |
| 7:00 - 8:20 AM: | 12/19-1/9/99 | Relax at airport, then board plane |
| 8:20 - Noon: | 1/9 - 3/5 | Fly home |
| Noon - 1:00 PM: | 3/5 - 3/20 | Arrive home for Christmas! |

In terms of planning for the year 1998, some of these themes can already be seen based upon the symbolism of the corresponding times in which events unfolded during the solar return. For instance, in the 8:30 - 9:15 AM time band, the children were upset, realizing it was Christmas Eve, and they were not home with the entire family (grandparents and cousins). This correlates with January 10 - 22 of 1998, a time when the author will be leaving to the Far East for a speaking tour. It could well be a time when the children - or family - may experience being upset because we are "apart" from one another. During the 10:05-10:40 time band, the author experienced a high degree of relaxation and pleasure, as he received a massage and chiropractic adjustment. This corresponds to the calendar time of February 4-13, 1998, a time when the author will be on the annual family vacation, relaxing at the family's time-share apartment in Marco Island, Florida. During the 4:00 - 5:00 PM time slot that day, the author did his annual "taped consultation" for which he gets paid. As mentioned previously, I always try to do at least one hour of work on my solar return, because it symbolizes making money for the year. This correlates with May 3-18, 1998, a time when the author will be conducting a financial market timing workshop. He will be traveling at this time, and interestingly enough, this taped consultation took place during the drive from Tucson to Phoenix. The drive itself took place between 3:30 - 6:00

PM, which coincides with April 26-June 3, 1998. It is also during that time that the author plans on driving from Michigan to the UAC conference in Atlanta (May 20-26).

This then concludes our case history examples from the author's personal files on how to "put it all together." In summary, a proper solar return involves the following features:

- Determine the subject's intentions for the year.
- Determine a location where the horoscope for that moment will support the realization of those intentions.
- Encourage the subject to plan an experience going into the time of the solar return that will symbolically reflect the positive unfoldment of those intentions.
- At the moment of the solar return, encourage the subject to find a quiet place to meditate, to visualize his/her goals and wishes for the year. It is important to be reverent for this moment.
- Plan activities during the 24 hours that follow the solar return that are pleasant, enjoyable, and avoid all stress if possible.
- Keep a diary of events and experiences that unfold 6 hours before through 30 hours after this solar return moment. Convert these times to calendar dates for the next year, to get an idea of what themes will evolve - and they will unfold - during this year.

With the understanding of astrology gleaned through this book, and with proper preparation for each solar return, one can assure that each year will be a very special year in life, and that each return will indeed be the joyous and sacred cosmic event that it is meant to be. Life is an adventure, and solar returns - done properly - become an annual pilgrimage that is part of one's spiritual heritage. With solar returns, life (the Sun) returns to the beginning point of one's cycle. With an awareness of solar returns, one has a deeper appreciation for his/her relationship to the Infinite.